ANTIQUE FURNITURE

A guide to collecting affordable

ANTIQUE FURNITURE

Caroline Wheater

VIVAYS PUBLISHING

Published by Vivays Publishing Ltd
www.vivays-publishing.com

A catalogue record for this book is available from the British Library

ISBN 978-1-908126-33-7

Publishing Director: Lee Ripley
Design Concept: Price Watkins
Design: Tiziana Lardieri

Cover: Courtesy of The Decorative Antiques and Textiles Fair
Frontispiece: © Helen Toresdotter

Printed in China

Contents

Introduction

Back in the 1990s when my husband and I were putting together our first home, our parents gave us some inexpensive pieces of furniture to get us started. There was an old Victorian stripped pine washstand – the china basin had long gone but in its place was a round pewter tray. This is my dressing table now, complemented by a small, hinged mahogany mirror of the same period that I picked up for around £60/€69/$96 a few years ago. We were also given an early Victorian pine desk standing on slender turned legs that has become our hall console table. The long drawer at the front is a little bit warped with age and the drying effects of central heating, but that just adds to the charm – it's perfect for storing things away.

With the passing of time we have bought and acquired more antique and vintage pieces: two 19th century pine chests of drawers, deep and spacious in mellow, honey-coloured wood unlike today's orange stained and knotty pine. There's also an Edwardian beech towel rack for the bathroom, and a bentwood hat stand that dates to the early 1900s.

Two of my favourite things are recently inherited: a beautiful oak desk of early 1960s origin, with dovetail joints, little cubby holes and a hidden drawer for stationery and bits and bobs. While it's not officially an antique, at under 100 years old, it is very well made and designed – better than anything I could buy on the High Street today. In our sitting room is a perfectly proportioned 1960s oak coffee table with magazine rack underneath. With 50 years of dusting, polishing and daily use it has taken on a rich colour and patina – that characteristic so prized by antiques dealers which only time can generate. These, I hope, will become heirlooms for the next generation to inherit.

Of course we have new furniture in our home too, but every time I see these old, well-loved items I feel a subtle sense of satisfaction. Not only are they attractive and functional, they also have a sense of history. When I visit historic houses and museums and see collections of lovely old antique furniture, my feelings are confirmed. While not everything is to my taste I like to look at the patina of the wood that has emerged over years of use, to imagine how a piece was placed and used by the owner, and to appreciate how fashionable it would have been at the time of its making.

For me, antique furniture has a place even in the most contemporary homes. There is a wealth of furniture available to buy at all price levels and the choice of period, style and finish is just as wide-ranging. Whether you have £100/€116/$160 to spend or £5,000/€5,800/$8,000 you'll find something to suit from antiques shops, centres, fairs and auctions across Britain, Europe and the USA. On the other hand you may be lucky enough to inherit some pieces that are already in the family.

Everyday antiques may not be the best of their type, or in the greatest condition – with the odd crack, shrinkage or wobble – but they are serviceable and solidly made, perfect for fitting out a first home. The more expensive pieces might appeal if your nest is empty and you can indulge your own tastes once more.

From these roots comes this book. I hope it inspires you to consider antique furniture afresh.

01

Why buy old?

Why buy old?

Our homes are our sanctuaries and furnishing them is a means of personal expression. But creating a warm and welcoming home is not an instant process: feathering one's nest can last a lifetime. Finding the perfect antique dining table may be a mission that takes several years, but will be worth the wait. Re-covering a cherished old sofa is an act of faith repaid in the comfort of the newly upholstered frame, built to last even if the original fabric wasn't. We may buy pieces of furniture to mark a significant life event, such as a house move, a special birthday or anniversary. Then, of course, there are the things we inherit from family, treasured pieces that are passed down through the generations.

Intriguing mix

To me, some of the friendliest, most interesting homes are those that have an informal mix of old and new furniture, giving rooms character and depth, a narrative as well as practicality and style. Blending new furniture with antiques creates a lived-in look that is not straight from the high street or out of a magazine, but reflects an individual interpretation of style and design.

As top interior designers know, this classic combination has a

double-edged reward, serving to enhance the freshness of the new while highlighting the inherent history and quality of the old. It's a winning formula for interiors experts such as Nicky Haslam, Tricia Guild and Martha Stewart, whose schemes, designs and ideas incorporate a range of old and new, seamlessly and with great style. To absorb some of that instinct for style, look at their latest books, visit their websites or potter round their emporiums.

This flexible approach to furnishing has another advantage: it enables you to accommodate inherited family pieces. Think carefully before you organise a clearance – could that wardrobe or chest of drawers or table fit into your own home, or that of a sibling or friend? Chances are that it is better made and of higher quality materials than you could buy new today. If in doubt, put it in storage for a few months while you decide.

*C*OLLECT IT: *APPRENTICE PIECES*

As you browse through shops and fairs looking at antiques you will inevitably come across miniature examples of furniture – tiny chests of drawers, gateleg tables, wardrobes and chairs for example. If finely made, these could be 'apprentice pieces', miniature versions of full-sized furniture made by apprentices before they become fully-fledged cabinet-makers. However, miniature furniture can also be samples made to drum up business, and prototypes produced by workshops. Whatever their provenance, these charming pieces look lovely on a mantelpiece, or for keeping jewellery on a dressing table, or for storing small items of stationery on a desk.

This turn-of-the-century oak bookcase has been lightened with specialist wood bleach to better suit a modern home. It has attractive astragal glazing – decorative wooden glazing bars which separate the glass panels. Use it to display ornaments, keep books or store ceramics, china and glass.

COLLECT IT: *CHILDREN'S FURNITURE*

Furniture made for children is a popular collectors' area. Such pieces are just the same quality as larger versions, but are charmingly small. Find Windsor chairs, rocking chairs, correction chairs (for disciplining schoolchildren to sit straight and still), slipper chairs and more. This beautiful little walnut 'show-wood' armchair is a fine example; dating to around 1860, it has been re-upholstered and is from J Collins & Son in Bideford, Devon (www.collinsantiques.co.uk).

Wide choice

Whether you prefer to buy in the environment of an antiques shop or centre, to visit fairs, or bid at auctions, there is much to entice. And the more comfortable you become with antique furniture, the more your taste will develop. Highly affordable everyday pieces include tables, chairs, sofas, mirrors and chests. For a budget of several thousand you can buy something really special such as a dresser, a grandfather clock, or a piece of Biedermeier furniture as a talking point for a room. Then there are all the quirky small pieces that are waiting to be snapped up: cutlery trays, stationery holders, whatnots, walking sticks, hand mirrors, hanging shelves and footstools. The opportunities are endless.

Oriental style has been popular in Britain since the 18th century when grand houses were decorated with hand-painted Chinoiserie wallpaper and expensive imported tea was drunk from delicate Chinese porcelain cups. As the Western fascination with the Orient continued, faux bamboo furniture became popular in late Victorian times. Made in London around 1880, this elegant faux bamboo desk has japanned decoration – layers of black lacquer painted with ornamental flowers and leaves

Compared to the often flimsy, self-assembly furnishings sold today, antiques offer a solid wood option for similar, if not cheaper, prices, and have a better resale value if you decide to change things around. There's no doubt that antiques have staying power. How can you not admire a piece of furniture that was made several centuries ago and is still standing – and looking rather good into the bargain? If your budget is tight, there is plenty of late 19th and early 20th century so-called 'brown' furniture that is of no particular merit, but is serviceable and easy to reinvent with a coat of satin finish paint or a new upholstery fabric.

There's no doubt that antiques have staying power

 BE INSPIRED: *THE FAIREST FAIR*

At top antiques fairs run by the trade associations BADA and LAPADA in Britain, and NAADAA in America, you will see some rare and beautifully crafted old furniture for sale, along with plenty more affordable pieces. Even if your budget is restricted these upmarket fairs are great places to get your eye in. Find out what's going on in your area via the umbrella organisation CINOA, which represents 5,000 dealers who are members of 32 antiques dealers' associations in 22 countries (www.cinoa.org).

Three styles of comfy Edwardian armchair have been given a new lease of life, recovered in vibrantly patterned, contemporary fabric

COLLECT IT: *COUNTRY OAK FURNITURE*

There is a long tradition of plain country furniture made in oak. Rustic furniture of this type can be expensive, which is why it pays to look outside major cities to source pieces. For example, this piece is from Country Oak Antiques, near Harrogate in Yorkshire, who concentrate on oak furniture from the 17th, 18th and 19th centuries, and try to keep their prices affordable. Owners Richard and Gillian Brown are experts in the history of this kind of furniture, which they sell from a former flax mill (www.countryoakantiques.co.uk).

Eco-friendly too

Environmentally, buying antiques makes sense too. When so many items have already been made using precious natural resources, why not cut your carbon footprint by investing in some of them? According to independent research commissioned by the Antiques Are Green Campaign (antiquesaregreen.org), a new piece of furniture with a lifespan of 15 years has a carbon footprint 16 times bigger than a 19th century antique with a 195-year lifespan. Buying 'old' is recycling at its best.

02

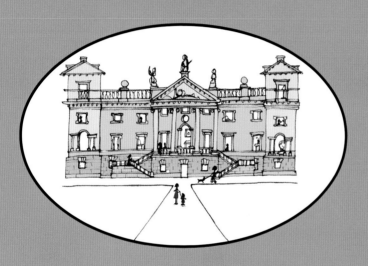

A dip into history

A dip into history

One of the oldest pieces of furniture in Britain is the Coronation Chair, made around 1300 at the order of King Edward I and kept in the Sacrarium of Westminster Abbey. Today, the gilded oak throne of surprisingly modest proportions and ornamentation has just been restored, readying it for several hundred years' more service. Amazingly, it has not fallen apart or rotted away, so well has it been cared for.

The Coronation Chair is an exceptional survivor and most 'old' furniture available to buy today is much younger. Fine pieces of furniture from the 1500s and 1600s endure – from the Elizabethan, Jacobean, Carolean and Restoration periods in Britain, the Renaissance in Europe, and the Early Colonial period in America – but much of it is in private hands or stately homes or museum collections, conserved for future generations to enjoy. It is to later centuries that we antiques buyers must look.

Furniture legacy

As the merchant classes grew in the 17th and 18th centuries, so did the demand for comfortable, well-made furniture. According to

research by London's Geffrye Museum of the Home, a typical 'hall' or main living room in a city merchant's house of 1630 was used daily for business, family leisure, dining and childcare. Consequently furniture had to be sturdily made to withstand family life, but look smart enough to impress visitors.

The living room would have been fashionably decked out with oak panelling, which also helped insulate the house from the cold in wintertime. Typical furniture would have included an oak dining table with extendable 'draw-leaves' to seat at least 10 people, stools and benches to sit upon, a fireside armchair for the head of the household or an honoured guest, and a court cupboard to keep and display pewter plates and tankards or earthenware ceramics such as Dutch and English Delftware.

One hundred years later, in 1735, the way people lived had evolved, becoming less formal and more varied and requiring different types of furniture. According to the Geffrye Museum of the Home, the living room was still used for family leisure and entertaining but not necessarily for dining, and was typically furnished with comfort in mind – upholstered, walnut wood chairs, a writing bureau for composing letters, an over-mantel mirror to reflect more light into the room, a stylish marble fireplace, and a small tripod table for serving newly fashionable tea.

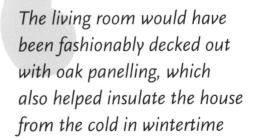

The living room would have been fashionably decked out with oak panelling, which also helped insulate the house from the cold in wintertime

A small 19th century sofa in Louis XV style would not look out of place today. It has been reupholstered in a light patterned fabric that sets off the stained beech 'show-wood' frame made to resemble more expensive walnut

A golden age for craftsmen

The previous scene is just one snapshot of how a family lived several centuries ago, but it illustrates how domestic furniture evolved and, as the 18th century continued, how designs proliferated. In Britain and abroad the Georgian era (1714–1800) was a celebrated age of craftsmanship championed by cabinet-makers (the term for fine furniture makers; traditionally, carpenters worked on roofs and floors while joiners fixed stairs and panelling). Renowned British cabinet-makers such as Thomas Chippendale, George Hepplewhite, Thomas Sheraton, George Seddon, and the partnership of William Ince and John Mayhew influenced furniture design as far afield as the USA.

Thomas Chippendale was the first British cabinet-maker to record his designs and make them available to others (at a price) when he published *The Gentleman and Cabinet-Maker's Directory* in 1754. Between 1759 and 1763 Ince and Mayhew published their design blueprints in the *Universal System of Household Furniture*, and from 1791 to 1794 Sheraton published his in the *Cabinet-Maker and Upholsterer's Drawing Book*. These pattern books enabled furniture to be recreated by city and rural workshops alike, with varying standards of end product.

The growing appetite for furniture encouraged cabinet-making businesses to open in the main towns and cities of Britain. There was strong demand for skilled cabinet-makers to craft pieces and these skills were often passed from father to son. It was common for boys at the age of 14 to become apprenticed for seven years until the age of 21 when they could begin to earn money as qualified craftsmen. An apprentice learned how to carve and turn wood, and how to construct furniture using precise techniques such as dovetail joints, and pegged mortise and tenon joints (the mortise is the hole, the tenon is the tongue of wood that fits in it, the peg holds the two together).

This Regency rosewood 'Canterbury' is a little piece of history, made to hold sheet music and journals. Sought after today by antiques lovers, a good quality Canterbury can command a high price

 HOT BUY: *ANTIQUE TABLES*

In the 17th century, tables were generally a simple affair, usually made of oak – perhaps a trestle, or a 'draw-leaf' extendable table, or a portable gateleg table, or even a coffer (chest) that doubled as a table. Within 200 years the family of table designs had grown to include wind-out extending dining tables, round tilt-top tables that folded up for ease of storage, revolving 'drum' tables for libraries, small tea, kettle and wine tables, occasional tripod tables, gaming tables, 'work' or sewing tables, nests of tables, desk tables, dressing tables and washstands.

Window seats were commonplace in well-to-do homes of the 18th and 19th centuries. This example, around 200 years old, is made of mahogany and has been reupholstered in a light blue fabric

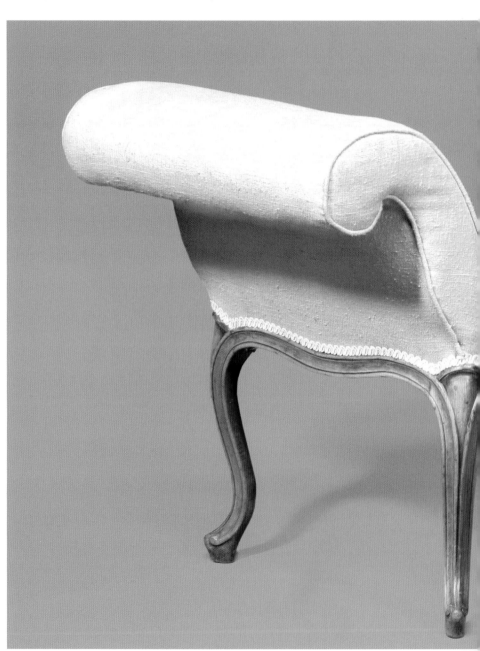

 BE INSPIRED: *ARTFUL RESEARCH*

To research how furniture was used in the past look at old paintings. You could visit an art museum, go through books on art or look at picture archives on the Internet. For example, there are plenty of 18th and 19th century paintings depicting domestic interiors. For inspiration search out pictures by artists such as the Englishman Sir John Everett Millais, the Swede Carl Larsson, the Dane Vilhelm Hammershoi, the German Johan Zoffany, Frenchmen Henri Matisse and Pierre-Auguste Renoir, Dutchman Johannes Vermeer and Americans Edmund Charles Tarbell and Daniel Garber. In addition, Beatrix Potter's children's books are full of beautifully illustrated pieces of furniture of the British Victorian and Edwardian eras.

Speeding up

In the mid-19th century there was a step change in furniture making as the invention of labour-saving steam-powered hammers and presses and other mechanised processes, such as machine carving and steam-bending wood against iron frames, enabled the production of furniture to reach a mass-market scale. Technical progress allowed companies to use standardised components to produce items at more affordable prices for the growing number of 'middling' households moving to suburban areas, lured by jobs and new housing. These households wanted good furniture, built to last, to furnish their homes with.

The sheer quantity of furniture made in the second half of the 19th century and the early 20th century makes many such antiques very affordable today. In addition, revivals of the Georgian, Regency and Gothic styles during this period offer buyers the chance to own furniture in a period style they like, but to pay less than they would for the 'real thing'. A top quality early Georgian wing chair, for example, could fetch an eye-watering £30,000/€35,000/$48,000, while a late 19th century 'Georgian-style' wing chair could cost only a couple of thousand in comparison. Canny antiques hunting enables you to get the look you want without the hefty price tag.

Neat, small and well furnished with drawers, the Davenport was a popular style of writing desk in the 19th century. This one, c1870, has a leather surface

 PAST TIMES: *RETAIL THERAPY*

From the mid-19th century buying furniture became even easier for customers with the birth of the department store. Au Bon Marché (now Le Bon Marché) on the Left Bank in Paris was operating as a department store by 1852, Liberty & Co in London's Regent Street in 1875; Gamage's in nearby Holborn opened in 1878, while Macy's in New York had become a large department store by 1877. In the furniture departments a wide selection of fashionable styles and types of furniture would have been available to browse. Liberty & Co in particular promoted handcrafted work, including Arts & Crafts furnishings.

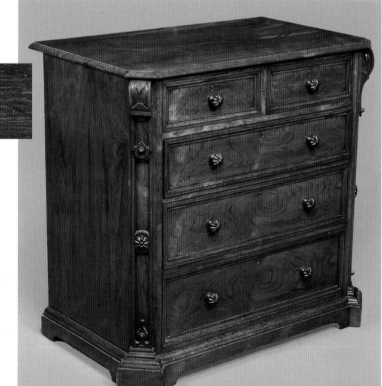

Made around 1835, this pretty rosewood chest of drawers is stamped 'GILLOW', indicating that it was made by the prestigious furniture makers Gillows of Lancaster. Such pieces are now highly collectable and command a premium. Other good names to look out for are Whytock & Reid and Maples from the 19th and early 20th centuries, and Heal's, Parker Knoll and Gordon Russell from the early to mid-20th century

A word on wood

These days much new furniture on offer is made from MDF or chipboard, also called particle board, covered with thin, machine-cut wood veneers. Cheaper solid woods such as pine, rubber wood and bamboo composites are popular too. The incontestable fact about antiques is that you get plenty of wood for your money, and often these woods are hard to come by today, either because they are now a protected species or have become very expensive.

Some (although not all) antique timber can be of a superior quality to that available today – trees cut down centuries ago were big and old and had a tighter, stronger grain. The girth of these great trees, particularly mahogany, meant that sawyers working in a sawpit – one man stood in the pit, the other stood above it to saw through the length of a wooden log – were able to cut wide planks from them to make into large tables and cabinets.

The finest quality wood was cut from the centre of the tree (sawing from top of log to bottom) closest to the heartwood where the grain is not as curved and therefore is less likely to warp as it dries. This technique was adapted in the late 1800s in America by the Arts & Crafts movement whose makers preferred to use 'quarter sawn' wood; in this case the log was cut vertically into quarters then the best planks cut from the centre of each quarter. Antique veneers are much thicker too, cut by hand rather than by machine as they are today; in addition they will be mounted on a less expensive, but real, wood, not on MDF or particle board as might be the case today.

Oak, a native wood in Britain, Europe and America, has always been used for both fine and country furniture. It is prized for being strong, easy to carve and durable. Walnut was another popular wood reserved for fine furniture, sometimes veneered on to a carcase of less expensive wood such as beech or pine. Another native northern-hemisphere tree, pine, provided wood for functional pieces such as farmhouse kitchen tables, chests of drawers and dressers. Ash, beech, elm and fruitwoods such as cherry and olive were commonly used too, plus birch in Scandinavian countries. American furniture makers could draw on a wide range of timbers from maple to white and red oak, cherry, beech, cedar, various pines, and black walnut.

By the 17th century, fine furniture makers were using exotic woods in their work, such as kingwood from Brazil. With its vibrant figure (markings) and colour, kingwood was made into only the very best and most expensive pieces – see rare examples at top antiques fairs today. While oak and walnut had been the mainstays of British furniture making well into the 18th century, from the 1730s another wood, mahogany, became available and was to become the dominant furnishing timber (in both solid and veneer forms) for over 150 years.

Some of the earliest, finest supplies of mahogany came from Jamaica, then part of the British West Indies. After Jamaican mahogany was exhausted new supplies were sourced from British Honduras (now Belize), Cuba, and Central and South America to satisfy demand from Britain and America. At the end of the 19th century African mahogany (from the related genus of tree, *Khaya*) became a major import.

Dark woods were very fashionable at the time and mahogany was favoured for its rich reddish-brown coloration and beautiful figure – some of the best mahogany has a 'flame' grain pattern visible on the surface. With a hard composition, the timber could be finely carved and highly polished to reflect daylight and candlelight into a room, as did glass chandeliers, mirrors and gilded furniture.

Oak, a native wood in Britain, Europe and America, has always been used for both fine and country furniture

In the 19th and early 20th centuries, oak and walnut regained popularity, while mahogany was joined by tropical hardwoods rosewood, tulipwood and satinwood. During this period less expensive woods such as beech were stained darker to resemble expensive rosewood – our ancestors were ever the pragmatists.

Visit any antiques centre or fair and you will find pieces made in all these woods. With a little restoration and sprucing up they look as good as, if not better than, the day they were made.

 INSTANT EXPERT: *WOOD WISE*

Antique furniture is made from a wide range of woods. All the woods in this checklist are hardwoods except pine and spruce, which are conifers and therefore softwoods.

ASH: Plain country furniture, often an element in Windsor chairs.
BEECH: Plain country furniture, prized for chair frames because upholstery nails do not split the wood. Often painted and also used as a carcase for more expensive walnut, mahogany and rosewood veneers.
BIRCH: Popular in Scandinavia and Eastern Europe, used to make Biedermeier furniture.
CHERRY: Fruitwood widely used in furniture making.
ELM: Simple country furniture, and often made into the seats of Windsor chairs.
MAHOGANY: Native to the West Indies, Central and South America, and related genus *Khaya* wood from Africa. First used by British furniture makers in the 1730s to 40s, mahogany was the dominant furnishing wood until the early 20th century, used as a

solid wood and as a veneer. What is referred to as 'true' mahogany from Central and South America is now rare and protected, with only African mahogany available in any amount to furniture makers.

MAPLE: Used widely in American antique furniture, its equivalent in Europe is sycamore. The finest 'tiger' or flame figured maple is much rarer than it was.

OAK: Ubiquitous in British, European and American furniture from the earliest times, in both country and finer furniture styles. Used as a carcase for expensive mahogany, walnut and rosewood veneers.

PINE: Including Scots pine, Baltic pine and North American pine – a blond wood widely used for basic country and utility furniture and as a carcase for more expensive wood veneers such as mahogany, walnut and rosewood; certain sizes of pine are sometimes referred to as 'deal'. Also made into serviceable furniture for kitchens and servants' quarters, and rooms away from public view, such as bedrooms. In this case it was usually painted, rather than left in its natural state, and much of what remains has been stripped.

ROSEWOOD: Native to South America, the muted brown wood that was used for the finest furniture, often as a veneer because of its high cost. Now a rare, protected species.

WALNUT: Used widely in furniture making, in solid form and as a veneer up until the mid-18th century, when mahogany became the fashionable wood. Walnut enjoyed a revival in the 19th century when it was used for the show-wood frames (visible wooden frames) of sofas and upholstered chairs.

(Opposite) These four late 18th century Hepplewhite-style chairs have shield-shaped backs and original painted decoration. Reupholstered in period-style fabric, they are in great condition

03

Buying antiques

Buying antiques

Given that shopping is an international pastime, browsing for antiques must be at the most pleasurable end of the scale. Sometimes there's nothing nicer than spending a few hours pottering around an antiques centre or street of small shops looking at a huge range of fascinating things and probably making at least one small purchase – I find old silver cutlery irresistible and highly affordable.

Antiques shops & centres

Before buying antique furniture it's helpful to get your eye in, and antiques shops offer the perfect opportunity to get a handle on price, check out the quality of construction and wood, take measurements and decide on what really appeals. Many dealers are knowledgeable and passionate about their subject and are more than happy to discuss a period or style. Any information you can glean about the provenance attached to a piece – who made it, who owned it, the history – adds to its value. Don't forget too that a good dealer often travels the length and breadth of the country to attend auctions and edit out the wheat from the chaff on behalf of customers. They will scan the auction catalogues every month and, out of the hundreds of

things on offer, will bid on just a handful of antiques that are good examples of their type. Many also source antiques from abroad or from out-of-the-way places and through specialist contacts built up over the years. This in-depth knowledge saves buyers time and money on travelling and searching.

While there are many decent dealers who don't belong to a trade association, it is always reassuring to know that you are buying from a dealer who subscribes to a code of conduct that has strict standards regarding authenticity and quality. The umbrella organisation CINOA lists antiques trade associations in 22 countries (www.cinoa.org to find out your regional associations). Browse respected dealers on the Internet too; www.onlinegalleries.com offers antiques from dealers based in over 21 countries.

With the economic environment tougher than ever, there has been a growth in antiques centres, gathering dealers together under one roof. The benefit of a centre is that there is a far greater range of antiques to choose from and browsing will reveal things that are new to you. I remember being delighted when I first saw a 'granddaughter' longcase clock, a comparatively short type of longcase clock made in the early 20th century.

Salvage yards are worth checking out, too. Although they specialise in reclaimed period building materials including bricks,

> *With the economic environment tougher than ever, there has been a growth in antiques centres, gathering dealers together under one roof*

flagstones, floorboards, tiles, gates and oddments like chimneypots and old signs, many of them also stock furnishings such as antique fireplaces, internal and external doors, door furniture, beds, benches, tables, baths and basins. Find reputable yards via SALVO, an international umbrella association of salvage dealers that provides details for specialists in the UK and other parts of Europe, the US and limited listings for many other countries (www.salvoweb.com).

If you're visiting an area for the first time, or on holiday, use the Internet to research local antiques centres and shops. By and large, in most towns there will be an antiques shop or two, but some towns teem with them. For example, Hungerford in Berkshire is home to the Hungerford Arcade, representing over 100 dealers, and one of the oldest antiques centres in the UK. Canonsburg in Pennsylvania, a small town near Pittsburgh, has more antiques shops per square mile than most large cities according to its website. In the south of France perhaps an hour's drive from Marseilles, L'Isle-sur-la-Sorgue has huge numbers of antiques shops. Antiques shops in well-heeled market towns may well yield good bargains, thanks to the supply of quality pieces obtained via local house clearances. The same is true in other European cities and towns.

Most towns have a website, setting out what they offer; some regions also have an antiques dealers' association, such as CADA (www.cotswolds-antiques-art.com), the Cotswold Art and Antique Dealers Association that represents dealers in 15 towns in the Cotswold area. Antiquars Antwerpen (www.antiquairs-antwerpen.be) lists dealers in Antwerp, and in Woodbury, Connecticut, the Woodbury Antiques Dealers' Association (www.antiqueswoodbury.com) offers guidance to their local dealers. These are but two more of the many such associations that exist, so do your research before you go. Then there are the antiques trade papers to pore over such as the UK's *Antiques Trade Gazette* and the US's *Antiques and the Arts Weekly*, and the website *Antiques News and Fairs* (www.antiquesnewsandfairs.co.uk).

Antiques fairs

Specialist antiques fairs are a great opportunity to meet up with a variety of dealers from all over the region, country, or abroad. You'll find everything from furniture to smaller collectables on offer. Typical stands range from upmarket retailers who usually operate from a shop, to small-scale dealers who don't have a shop or sometimes even a website, so catch them while you can. Some stand-holders only appear at a few fairs every year, building up stock between each one – so check with them if you're undecided about a piece: it might be your only chance to buy in six months.

The majority of fairs are small to medium size and offer a tailored selection of dealers. A select few are much larger, occupying show grounds or exhibition halls to accommodate the wares of hundreds of different dealers. A lot of the popular fairs run several times a year, so you can always go back once you've got the hang of it and found dealers you like – see the Fairs Calendar in Chapter 10 for more information.

If you're thinking of purchasing large items, travel by car so that you can take them home with you straight away. And take blankets to cushion purchases against bumps while on the road. Some fairs will offer a discount entry fee for group bookings, so consider organising an outing if you belong to a local club. And why not turn your visit into a weekend away? Antiques fairs are often held in interesting and picturesque surroundings, with locations close to historic houses and gardens, which is another good reason for taking time over planning a trip.

(Opposite) Antique chairs await reupholstery and are on sale for very reasonable prices from The Antique French Chair & Sofa Company at the Salvo Fair, Britain's biggest annual salvage event

Auction houses

Buying at auction

Auction houses mainly attract dealers but have become more accessible to the general public in recent years. If buying at auction appeals there are big auction houses in most major cities, but also plenty of regional and country auction houses to investigate. Some have catalogues with images available on their websites, so you can view items before the sale. If attending an auction is difficult, it is usually possible to bid by phone or in some cases over the Internet.

Really, though, there is no substitute for going to the auction house in person and viewing the lots on sale at the preview, held several days beforehand. Auction houses themselves strongly advise bidders to inspect items before bidding. This way you can see the proportions of a piece and check the quality of its design, construction, materials and current condition.

If you want to find out more about a particular antique, whether

Two of a set of five mid-19th century dining chairs made of mahogany, which sold at auction for
£220/€255/$350

it has undergone any restoration for example, ask the auctioneer specialists for further advice. Bear in mind that should furniture need conservation work done on it, this can be expensive. Ultimately, it is up to the buyer to be satisfied that an antique is worth bidding for and to set an upper limit that they are prepared to pay. Be aware that hammer prices can sometimes rise well above guide prices if competition for a piece is keen or prices have been pitched low to start with, to generate interest.

To buy at auction you will have to register with the auction house and provide an address to which the invoice will be sent, plus have official proof of identity to hand if needed. Telephone and Internet bidders will also have to register. Purchasers are required to pay a 'buyer's premium' on top of the hammer price, usually between 20 and 25 per cent of the price. Depending on what country you are in, there may also be sales tax applicable on the hammer price of some items. And remember, when the auctioneer's hammer has come down for the final time, the item is legally sold to the highest bidder.

BUYER'S TIP: *CHECK OUT CHARITY FURNITURE STORES*

House clearances are a potential source of antiques and vintage furniture. Often family haven't got room for old, quality furniture passed down by parents and donate it to a charity to sell through their furniture stores. Check websites for details of furniture stores run by hospices and charities such as the Red Cross, Oxfam, the British Heart Foundation, Humana, and Housing Works. And keep an eye out for bargains.

Selling at auction

Primarily the auction house acts on behalf of the seller, but sellers too will be charged a commission of around 15 per cent on the hammer price. To get a valuation for an antique you can send in photographs and a description to your chosen auction house, but the expert will probably want to see the piece in person. In the case of large, hard-to-move items, the expert will come out to your location to give a valuation.

The sale terms can vary from: having no reserve (minimum price) so that the piece goes to the highest bidder; to a discretionary sale whereby the auctioneer will sell the antique for 10 to 20 per cent below an agreed figure if necessary; to an agreed reserve sale whereby the piece will be sold for the reserve price or above. If your piece remains unsold, you will pay a small set fee and can either re-offer it in a forthcoming sale, or collect it to bring home.

INSTANT EXPERT: *TOP PLACES TO BUY IN LONDON*

- Kensington Church Street, W8 (www.antiques-london.com)
- Lillie Road, SW6 (www.lillieroad.co.uk)
- Portobello Road, W10 (www.portobelloroad.co.uk)
- Gray's Antiques Market, 58 Davies Street, W1 (www.graysantiques. com)
- Alfie's Antique Market, 13–25 Church Street, NW8 (www.alfiesantiques. com)

TOP PLACES TO BUY IN PARIS

- Carré Rive Gauche, 16 rue des Saints-Pères, 7th arrondissement, facing the Louvre (www.carrerivegauche.com)
- Le Village Suisse, 58 avenue de Suffren, 7th arrondissement, next to St Germain district (www.villagesuisse.com)
- Marchés aux Puces de St-Ouen – Porte de Clignancourt, rue des Rosiers, 18th arrondissement (www.marchesauxpuces.fr)
- Quai Voltaire, 7th arrondissement, close to St Germain district
- Village Saint-Paul, rue St Paul, 4th arrondissement, in the Marais district (www.village-saint-paul.com)

TOP PLACES TO BUY IN NEW YORK

- Circa Antiques, 374 Atlantic Avenue, Brooklyn, NY 11217 (www.circaantiquesltd.com)
- Long Island Exchange, 4338 Austin Boulevard, Island Park, NY 11558 (www.longislandantiques.com)
- Obscura Antiques & Oddities, 280 East 10th Street, NY 10009 (www.obscuraantiques.com)
- The Antiques Garage, West 25th Street Market, Hell's Kitchen Flea Market, New York (www.hellskitchenfleamarket.com)
- The Manhattan Art & Antiques Center, 1050 Second Avenue at 56th Street, NY 10022 (www.the-maac.com)
- Warren Street, City of Hudson, nr New York (www.hudsonantiques.net)

An Arts & Crafts chair of around 1900 is made of dark stained beech and oak, and has a simple rush seat; its auction estimate was £200–300/€232–350/$320–480

At approximately two and a half metres wide and tall, this 19th century breakfront bookcase in solid oak has already lasted several lifetimes and reached a price of £1,800/€2,100/$2,900 at auction

 INSTANT EXPERT: *AUCTION SAVVY*

- If possible, go to the sale preview before deciding to bid for a piece. Unless you have built up some expertise and know exactly what you're looking for, buying sight unseen can lead to disappointment.
- Take note of measurements and make sure furniture will fit in the room you have in mind, plus the doorways it will have to be brought through once it's back home.
- If you're on a budget and have a practical bent, look for cheap, run-of-the-mill antiques that need a little fixing and perhaps a spot of transformation such as painting, liming or bleaching (using a specialist wood bleach) to tone down dark wood.
- Remember that the hammer price will have a 20 to 25 per cent 'buyer's premium' added to the final bill, and possibly sales tax.
- Work out how you will transport the item home – check the price of delivery with the auction house if necessary.

Purchasing antiques online

Increasingly antiques shops and centres are offering items online, often on collective websites such as www.sellingantiques.co.uk or iantiqueonline.ning.com in the US. Here you can compare and contrast furniture, or source something from an antiques shop that's hard to get to. eBay is another marketplace for buying and selling antiques, and can yield finds. Sellers are a mix of private individuals and dealers who find eBay a more economical way of doing business. Always check out delivery arrangements and a seller's rating before you commit, also whether a piece can be returned or not. Again, with eBay you have to hope your bid wins or pay the asking price, but there are no guarantees that what you've set your heart on will become yours.

A word on prices

There's a perception that antique furniture is expensive, yet prices are the lowest they have been for over a decade, so this is a great time to buy. The sort of furniture highlighted in this book has price tags ranging from £100–5,000 ($160–8000/€120–5800), with lots in between to suit every budget. In most cases it would be hard to find a modern equivalent, made of solid wood or wood veneers, for the same price.

Age doesn't necessarily confer a high price because value is dependent on overall quality of wood and craftsmanship, plus the current desirability of a piece and whether a type of furniture is in fashion now. A piece of furniture that hasn't been altered over the years, which has had little restoration work and has kept all its original period features such as handles, feet and locks will be worth more than a similar example that has been restored and had features replaced. Dealers are always looking for items with original detailing, such as paint (however flaky), or leather (however scratched), because they fetch better prices.

There is no such thing as a definitive price either; it depends where you buy from, what a dealer or auction house is prepared to take for an item, and in general terms what the local market will bear. Auction houses can yield some great buys if you're prepared to throw your hat into the ring, but then so can local antiques shops and centres. The best advice is to look around and do your homework on the range of prices offered before making a purchase.

The best advice is to look around and do your homework on the range of prices offered before making a purchase

If buying at auction, look at the results of recent past sales to see price levels reached for similar items; in the UK you can follow live auctions, and even bid if the fancy takes you, at the website www.the-saleroom.com. If hunting around shops or fairs, take in a few dealers before you make a decision. A dealer may be prepared to offer a reduction on the quoted price of up to ten per cent, so ask them for their 'best price' before sealing the deal.

An Edwardian *bonheur du jour* (lady's writing desk) in mahogany with inlay sold for £500/€580/$800 at auction

 **ANTIQUES HOTSPOT:**

TOULOUSE, FRANCE

The terracotta landscape of La Ville Rose (the 'pink city') is a great place to weekend. After visiting the Romanesque Basilica Saint-Sernin and the wonderful food market at Marché Victor Hugo, set aside some time to go antiquing. On Rue Fermat check out Joan Pujol et Patrick Martin, renowned for large-scale marble and wood antique furniture; Bibliothèques Anciennes, stocked with books, chests, bookcases and *armoires*; and Le Petit Detail for handcrafted items such as throws, lamps and ceramics. And on the corner of secluded Place Saintes Scarbes is Lieu de Charme, a *brocante* that sells vintage desks, prints and metal shelving. Time your trip the first weekend of every month and you'll be able to visit the city fleamarket on Allées Jules Guesde.

THE COTSWOLDS, UK

The Cotswolds has the largest concentration of antiques dealers outside London, based in towns such as Tetbury, Broadway and Chipping Campden. Other highlights include Burford, where Antiques@The George at 104 High Street, a former coaching inn that welcomed Nell Gwynne and King Charles II, is now a creaky-floored antiques centre filled with interesting and affordable furniture and trinkets. Manfred Schotten offers an unrivalled selection of sporting antiques. Then there's lovely Stow-on-the-Wold. On Sheep Street you'll find Christopher Clarke Antiques, a specialist in campaign furniture and 'travelling' items such as binoculars, candlesticks and cocktail shakers. Check out Styles of Stow too, and the American-owned Durham House Antiques centre which represents 30 dealers.

HARROGATE, YORKSHIRE, UK

As well as being the birthplace of famous Betty's café and tea rooms in 1919, Harrogate has lots of interest for antiques hunters. In the Montpellier Quarter, which dates to Georgian times, you'll find Paul Wetherell Antiques with a good selection of fine furniture, and nearby Montpellier Mews Antique Market representing over 25 dealers. At Elaine Phillips Antiques on Royal Parade find

English oak, mahogany and walnut furniture of the 17th and 18th centuries plus plenty of ideas on how to use antiques in a contemporary setting. At an 18th century former coaching inn at nearby Pateley Bridge visit David South who specialises in reupholstering period sofas, chaises longues and armchairs. Choose from stock already renewed or pick your own fabric for a piece of your choosing.

EDINBURGH, SCOTLAND

A gem of a city for sightseeing and shopping, Edinburgh offers plenty in the way of antiques, too. Head to the elegant New Town to find Unicorn Antiques at 65 Dundas Street, a former dairy now crammed with antiques, ranging from Victorian cut crystal, clocks and cutlery to larger items including mirrors, paintings, curtain poles and small furnishings. A little way out of town at Leith Links is Georgian Antiques, housed in an old whisky bond. Stock is laid out over five floors and most visitors come for the Georgian and Victorian furniture, particularly pieces made by the renowned Edinburgh firm of Whytock & Reid. Cabaret Antiques at 137 West Port, beneath Edinburgh Castle, offers smaller items of furniture plus antique jewellery, glass and ceramics.

A 19th century mahogany linen press comprising two parts, a cupboard and drawers sitting one upon the other, fetched £1,000/€1,160/$1,600 at auction

04

Everyday antiques I:
seating and dining

Everyday antiques I: seating and dining

The antiques highlighted in this chapter and the one following are just the tip of the iceberg as you'll discover when you go out antiques hunting, and are all 100 years old or more. Browse any antiques shop, fair or auction and you will be surprised by the variety of shapes, styles, periods and purposes of antique items available. This selection aims to whet your appetite for more discoveries and bargaining of your own, and ranges from items that cost from around £100/€116/$160 up to several thousand.

Generally speaking, quality will out, which means that the overall condition, timber type and quality of craftsmanship will always be reflected in the price of an antique. Other factors include rarity and whether or not this type of furniture is currently in fashion. If you're investing, spend as much as you can afford, but if bargains are your bag prepare to be pleasantly surprised at how far your money will stretch.

Seating

Chairs

A pair of 1830s French mahogany *fauteuils* in Empire style – a type of chair known as 'open elbow' in England

What a wonderful piece of furniture the chair is. It can be practical and made for a purpose such as dining; designed for comfort and relaxation; or just plain stylish. The chair has had so many guises over the centuries that there is surely a type to please every taste. Consider buying a single chair for your hall, kitchen, living room or bedroom. Around the dining table, a set of 'harlequin' or non-matching chairs can be a talking point among your guests and a pleasure to hunt for. A single chair can cost from under £100/€116/$160 at auction, a well-preserved set of chairs in good condition may cost up to £2,000/€2,300/$3,200 bought at an antiques fair – the choice is wide and eclectic.

William & Mary armchair

Made in the reign of joint monarchs William and Mary (1688–1702), this rather sober style of chair has a high back, turned legs, S-shaped arms, and is topped off with decorative carved acanthus leaves and C-scrolls. It's a piece to admire for its craftsmanship, and is of a genre often seen in historic houses. This chair fetched £400/€465/$640 at auction but would command more once restored.

Regency armchair

This shapely mahogany armchair, c1815, is designed in Neo-classical style, popular during the Regency period (roughly 1800 to 1830, when the British Prince Regent, later George IV, was influential on fashion). It was probably part of a set of dining chairs and has scrolling arms and sabre-shaped legs, and is decorated with carved swirls of foliage. The fabric seat cover is a later addition, which lessens its value – original features will always push up the price. Desirable for its Regency looks, at auction it sold for £300/€348/$480.

Victorian hall seat

This upholstered leather chair was made around 1860 and embodies the impressive, masculine character of mid-Victorian furniture. Hall seats were for the use of visitors and servants when making calls to households. The chair's chunky oak framework supports a 76cm/30in wide seat, but is narrow enough not to be an obstacle in the hallway. It may well have been teamed with a hallstand, a practical piece of furniture that combined a mirror, pegs for coats, and a drip tray for umbrellas. Whether it is put in a hall or elsewhere today, it remains a noteworthy feature. This one sold for £260/€300/$415 at auction, lucky buyer!

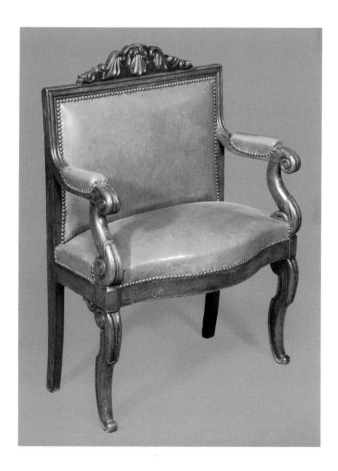

Victorian library chair

This solid walnut wood chair dates to around 1880, when free public libraries began opening in Britain and America. Philanthropists such as American Andrew Carnegie and local councils in the UK were the driving forces behind bringing books to the wider public. Library users needed chairs that were comfortable to sit in for possibly hours at a time, hence the leather upholstery and curved, padded leather back. These days, library chairs are very popular and fetch good prices at auction (this one, £350/€405/$560) and in antiques shops.

Victorian bergère armchair

With a framework of mahogany, this mid-19th century caned *bergère* chair has interesting details including reeded tapering legs, which hark back to Georgian style. It may once have been part of a set. Cane has been used as a seating material since the 17th century and the French word 'bergère' means an armchair with an enclosed back and arms; the opposite style is a 'fauteuil' or 'open elbow' armchair. *Bergères* are perennially popular, reflected in the auction hammer price of £380/€440/$605.

Edwardian painted chair

This early 20th century painted chair with an arch back reflects the revival of medieval Gothic style in the 19th century, which inspired authors of romantic literature, architects and designers. This very Victorian fashion can be seen on a grand scale at the Houses of Parliament in Westminster, in the exterior designed by George Gilbert Scott and in the interior created by Augustus Pugin. This chair is an unusual piece and the fair price tag of £780/€905/$1,250 reflects its individuality.

Set of 19th century dining chairs

Dating to around 1840, these five dining chairs have rosewood frames, a fashionable choice of timber for early Victorian dining chairs. The chairs have the classic 'balloon-back' shape and are carved with floral motifs called anthemion, and the seats are cane. Sets of chairs usually command higher prices than singles, but this set went for a highly competitive £200/€230/$320 at auction. Expect to pay considerably more for larger and even-numbered sets of chairs.

French occasional chairs

These understated occasional chairs were made in France around 1770. As their name suggests, they were placed in rooms used for entertaining and leisure, where the household would socialise or the women of the family would withdraw to sew, sketch, write letters and read. French salon chairs are always popular and the fact that this set still has its original paint means the chairs can command a price of £2,000/€2,320/$3,200 at an antiques fair.

Victorian nursing chair

Nursing chairs were commonplace in the 19th century and enabled the nurturing of babies in comfort. This is a nice example with a mahogany show-wood frame and cabriole legs, plus a generously proportioned seat and back. At auction it fetched just £70/€80/$110, perhaps because the fabric lets it down.

     Slipper chairs, designed for the bedroom, are similar in style – low slung, with a long back to support the sitter. Such chairs are great value at the moment.

Stools

Stools have always been popular: simply designed, space-saving and portable. Antiques range from three-legged kitchen and dairy stools to more sophisticated window stools, music stools and footstools so popular in the 18th and 19th centuries. Most upholstered stools found today will have been recovered in new fabric. You'll find versions in painted wood, with caned seats, in mahogany, oak and walnut, and with all kinds of differently shaped legs and feet. Keep your eyes open for these small but charming furniture treasures that can be bought for under £100/€115/$160 at antiques shops and centres.

Victorian tuffet

This plain but pretty tuffet, or footstool, would have been a common sight in 19th century homes, providing a comfy rest for slippered feet warming in front of an open fire. The word tuffet entered popular parlance via the 1805 nursery rhyme, 'Little Miss Muffet', who sat on a tuffet. With a stained beech frame to resemble mahogany or walnut, this example has a removable cushion top that has been recovered in dark green silk. Small antique footstools such as this can be found from £80/€93/$128 upwards at antiques centres.

19th century window seats

If you like the novels of Jane Austen, you'll recall that window seats were essential to keep watch for visitors. This pair of window seats was made in the 19th century, but in late 18th century style, with classic sabre front legs and high end scrolls to each side.

They have been reupholstered in a pretty Regency-style striped fabric. The wood is unidentified but could be beech or pine, stained dark to resemble mahogany, a practice in the furniture trade that kept prices down. While this pair fetched £380/€440 /$610 at auction, once restored and buffed up they would be worth more.

19th century upholstered stool

This substantial 19th century stool is made from walnut wood and was probably designed for a library or a gentleman's club. The original leather seat bears stains and the cabriole legs have a timeworn patina

– but these are considered authentic signs of age, so desirable: probably why the stool fetched a healthy £390/€450/$625 at auction.

Sofas

Sofas, settees, day beds and chaises longues are all descended from wooden benches and settles, furniture that allowed several people to sit together in comfort. Inspired by stylish French interiors, elegant salon sofas in Neo-classical style became a furniture staple in the grand 18th century houses of Britain and America. By the 19th century, the fashion had filtered down to middle-class households too. The coiled spring was patented in 1828, and by the 1830s was widely used to create a more luxurious feel with deeper stuffing, emphasised by the use of buttoning. Many examples have 'show-wood' frames, where the timber frame is visible. Antique sofas can be picked up for considerably less than the price of a brand new sofa, but for the best pieces that have been restored and recovered in designer fabric, prices can rise to several thousand.

Victorian day bed

With mahogany legs and button upholstery this day bed was made around 1870, allowing the owner to rest up in elegant fashion during the day. With a new fabric cover it looks as good as new, and at two metres long really does what it says – providing a comfortable base on which to doze. Perfect for a large bedroom or living room, and a smidge under £500/€580/$800 at auction.

Antique sofas can be picked up for considerably less than the price of a brand new sofa

Victorian S-shaped chaise longue

A chaise longue means 'long chair' in French, suitable for resting with legs and feet up. The wooden frame of this chaise is made of versatile beech, stained to resemble more expensive mahogany or walnut. The S-shape is perhaps a harbinger of the Art Nouveau style, which became popular towards the end of the 19th century, with its famous 'whiplash curve' motif. This unusual chaise was given a guide price of between £600–800/€700–930/$960–1,300 at auction.

19th century American-style sofa

Made in the mid 19th century, this chunky, stubby sofa has an impressive mahogany framework and plump upholstery – clearly a piece made to impress, and one inspired by earlier Neo-classical American designs. The wood has a highly figured, rich patina with some decorative carving. The fabric cover is a replacement for the original. Perhaps it was owned by an American living in Britain? Unusual and in good condition, it had a guide price at auction of between £800/€930/$1,300 and £1,200/€1,400/$1,920.

Late 19th century camel-back sofa

As with other 19th century furniture, the design of this French sofa was inspired by the previous century's style and echoes a popular sofa shape known as the 'camel back'. Dating to around 1890 or 1900, the large sofa has been fully restored and reupholstered using good quality stuffing and a luxurious fabric, and as such had a price of £2,500/€2,900/$4,000 at a fair.

Early 19th century Baltic sofa

With its design inspired by the elegant, restrained style of
Scandinavia, this classy sofa has all the plain and simple attributes to
fit well into a contemporary setting. It dates to around 1800 and is
made of mahogany with decorative brass inlay. At under
£1,800/€2,100/$2,900 at a fair, its price compares well with the cost
of a large modern sofa.

Tables

Small tables

In the 18th century, as people began to entertain at home more, table designs diversified to accommodate all sorts of pursuits, from serving tea, wine and hot chocolate to playing cards, sewing, drawing and letter-writing. Portability was a feature of the small occasional table, typified by the popular tripod table with a tilt top that could be neatly stored against a wall when not in use. Today small antique tables are ideal for serving drinks and nibbles, for the bedside or for placing lamps on, while the larger examples would make a perfect kitchen table. Pick them up from a couple of hundred pounds/euros/dollars to a thousand and occasionally more, depending on quality and desirability.

Late 18th century oak tripod table

Made around 1780, this tripod table took up little space and was easily moved around a room. This version would have been used to serve tea, then a fashionable pastime. Made in oak, it is a country piece, but with a baluster stem and elegant pad feet that were typical of 18th century style. It sold at auction for £150/€175/$240; little tables such as these are perennially popular.

Late 18th century piecrust edge table

So popular were tripod tables in the 18th century that they became an essential household item, for both serving tea and for use as occasional tables. This neat mahogany version, crafted around 1770, has a rich patina that reveals its age – a contributing factor to its fetching £240/€280/$385 at auction. The Rococo-style carved piecrust edge around the tabletop prevents things from falling over the edge. It has French-style, curving cabriole legs and understated pad feet.

Late 19th century marquetry occasional table

With its serpentine shape and cabriole legs, this petite table and drawers looks Georgian but is in fact late 19th century/early 20th century in period. At this time there was a revival in late Georgian and early Regency furniture designs, so buying a 'younger' piece can be a way of getting the look or the original era without paying the premium that usually entails. Made from harewood and with marquetry detail, it fetched £550/€640/$880 at auction.

Early 19th century work table

At 70cm/27.5in high, this compact work table is the height of today's average desk, so comfortable to sit at. Dating to around 1800, it is constructed from mahogany and sits on casters for ease of moving around. Work tables were designed for sewing at, and came in all shapes and sizes – this example has a small pull-out desk flap and three slim drawers. A lovely period detail is the 'candle slide', a flat wooden support which pulls out for placing a candlestick holder upon – perhaps the reason it sold for £750/€870/$1,200 at auction.

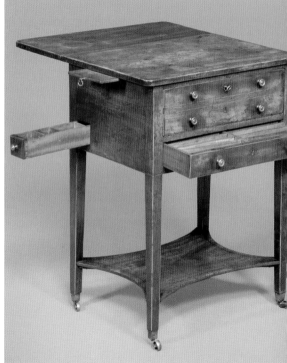

Late Victorian Japanese-style table

This small table with parcel gilt decoration is made from wood that has been ebonised, or stained black, following the fashion in Britain in the 1870s and 1880s for Japanese black lacquered furniture. Ebony itself is a dense, dark wood from West Africa and Southeast Asia that was used to make luxury carved cabinets, hence the term *ébéniste*, the French word for cabinet-maker. At auction this example fetched £250/€290/$400, but unusual, decorative occasional tables such as this usually command a premium at fairs.

Nest of four occasional tables

The design for a nest of occasional tables first became popular in France in the 18th century, providing elegant, portable surfaces that required little storage space when not in use. The idea caught on and nests in one guise or another have been with us ever since. Although this nest, painted with bucolic rural scenes, reproduces the French 18th century style, it was made around 1900. The tallest table is 72cm/28.3in high and ideal for placing a vase of flowers on. Desirable nests can sell for well over £1,000/€1,200/$1,600 retail, but will be more affordable at auction – the guide price for this set was £400–600/€465–700/$640–960.

Late Victorian butler's tray

For fans of costume drama on television, the butler's tray will be a familiar piece of furniture. The large, sturdy tray was used to carry food into the dining room where it was set on top of folding legs; sometimes a tray had collapsible sides so that it resembled a table. This painted wood butler's tray dates to around 1880 and has an attractive 'pierced gallery' or edge to prevent things from falling off. Butler's trays vary wildly in price, but you're unlikely to find one for less than £250/€290/$400 at a fair or shop, and this would be for a basic, late Victorian version; a Georgian butler's tray could easily sell for £750/€870/$1,200.

19th century Chinoiserie occasional table

Chinoiserie decoration inspired by Chinese motifs has remained perennially popular down the centuries. This pretty little table from the Regency period has a black lacquerwork ground on which are painted scenes of a family in a beautiful garden. The decoration is an example of penwork – a method of applying colour using quill pens then sealing and protecting the surface with varnish. Unusual and desirable; the asking price was £950/€1,100/$1,520 at a fair.

Large tables

At high-end antiques fairs you will see some truly beautiful, large mahogany tables from the 18th and early 19th centuries, an object lesson in craftsmanship. Of course, they have a price tag to match – think £50,000/€58,000/$80,000 and above. Fortunately, there are plenty more affordable tables to consider, especially from the Victorian period, with pine tables available from around £500/€580/$800 and more formal extendable tables for £1,000/€1,200/$1,600 or so. Decide your budget and see what it will get you.

18th century drop-leaf dining table

The Georgians were very practical and keen on stowing things away, as this well proportioned mahogany dining table, made around 1760, shows. The drop-leaf dining table was a forerunner of the extending table, with both outer leaves folding down when not in use. On turned legs and with pad feet, this table would benefit from some restoration work, which is why its auction guide price was £400–£600/€465–700/$640–960.

19th century dining table

We always tend to think of antique furniture as being big, but as this elegant mahogany dining table shows, that is not always the case. At 122cm/48in long and 100cm/39.3in wide it would have served as a breakfast table. Now, it is ideal for use in a small dining area or a large study. Made around 1800, the wooden tabletop has a rich patina and stands on downswept legs. Plus, set on casters, it's easy to move around. The auction guide price was £400–£600/€465–700/$640–960.

Regency sofa table

The sofa table was popularised in Britain by Sheraton in the late 18th century, and was positioned behind a sofa for reading, drawing and letter-writing – such tables have short flaps on either side to increase the surface space. This mahogany version, dating to 1815, has two drawers to the front and two false drawers on the reverse, with a generous top that is 140cm/55in long. The elegant, pared-down lines of Regency furniture suits today's interiors, and sofa tables in good condition can fetch good prices; this one was £950/€1,100/$1,520 at auction.

19th century Pembroke table

The Pembroke table is another classic design of the mid-18th century onwards and was used to serve an informal breakfast, tea or supper. The name is thought to derive from the Countess of Pembroke who is said to have ordered one of the early examples. In this version the drawers would have housed table linen (traditionally referred to as napery), and the two flaps on either side created a generous square shape, suitable for one or two diners. In today's world it would happily seat four and fit into a smallish dining area. It fetched £450/€520/$720 at auction.

18th century drum table

This small drum table has a leather top, akin to a desk. As a type, drum tables were introduced in the mid-18th century to hold paperwork. By the 19th century they had migrated into the library. The wonderful thing about a drum table is that the top revolves, making the drawers easily accessible to the person working at it. These days drum tables are popular for putting into spacious halls, or even for use as dining tables. They are on the pricey side – this one cost £4,800/€5,570/$7,680 at a fair – but then they have a unique look and an interesting story.

Victorian pine table

The plain pine table has a long and illustrious domestic history. This example, over 2m/6.5ft long, is a Victorian scullery table that would have been used to prepare vegetables, stack up plates and store kitchen cutlery, probably in the basement kitchen of a moderately well-off household. Its well-scrubbed top shows it has had plenty of wear. These days it would make a lovely kitchen or rustic-looking dining table, with plenty of space for all the family; and at an auction price of £750/€870/$1,200, it wouldn't break the bank. There are many styles of pine table to choose from, including chunky English and French farmhouse tables, and long, thin French 'harvest' tables, used for the celebratory meal at the end of the autumn grape harvest.

05

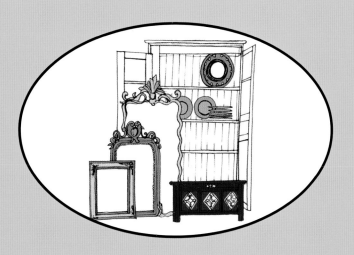

Everyday antiques II: mirrors and storage

Everyday antiques II: mirrors and storage

A s in the previous chapter, these everyday items are just some examples of the wide range you can find as you visit antique shops and centres. Antiques are often more decorative and ornamental than similar contemporary pieces, but the extra detail adds to their appeal and gives them authenticity. There's nothing like the soft gleam of an antique mirror when compared to its harsh aluminium-coated descendent.

Mirrors

In the 18th century mirrors were a luxury, with reflective tin-mercury amalgam surfaces and gilded frames. In grand houses, drawing rooms and salons were furnished with huge over-mantel mirrors above fireplaces, and tall pier glasses mounted on the wall spaces between windows to reflect light back into the room. On a smaller scale people used tabletop dressing glasses and long cheval mirrors to dress.

In the 1800s mirrors became more widely available. Traditionally the frames were made from lime wood or cheaper pine, both of which are easy to carve. Layers of gesso, a mixture of whiting and rabbit skin

glue, would be applied to the frame to hide the wood grain and to make a smooth surface for gilding with gold leaf. The best, most sought-after mirrors display hand-carved wooden details such as cherubs, flowers and foliage, but the majority are decorated with cast composite – a solid blend of gesso, rabbit-skin glue and linseed oil that was set in ornamental moulds then attached to the frame.

In 1840 the use of mercury amalgams was banned and makers used silver plate until the mid-20th century when aluminium-based reflective coatings were introduced. That is why old mirrors with original glass have a softer tone and why collectors love to see the foxing and chipping that show a mirror's true age. Hand mirrors can be picked up for £20/€23/$32, with plenty more late Victorian mirrors around £100/€115/$160, while older, rarer wall mirrors can fetch prices in the high hundreds.

A charming early 20th century blue lacquer cheval mirror

18th century wall mirror

With a frame made in walnut that has developed a beautiful patina over the centuries, and decorated with parcel gilt (part-gilded), this crested mirror dates to around 1740. At just under 1m/3.3 ft high and 50cm/19.7in wide, it is no shrinking violet and would look bold in a hallway. Although the frame is authentic, the mirror glass cannot be vouched for, and is likely to be a later replacement made of silver plate, rather than the tin-mercury amalgam used in the 18th century. At auction it fetched £420/€490/$670.

Edwardian cheval mirror

Invented in the 18th century, full-length cheval mirrors were adjustable so that the mirror could be angled upwards or downwards. The support mechanism was called a 'horse', hence the French word for horse, *cheval*, being used to describe this type of mirror. Here, an Edwardian mahogany and satinwood version, c1910, is made in a late 18th century style in a shield shape (chairs were also made with shield backs). Good quality cheval mirrors are desirable, and this one fetched the solid price of £600/€695/$960 at auction; expect to pay more in a shop.

Regency dressing glass

Dainty dressing glasses, or mirrors, were placed on chests or small tables for women to do their toilette, put on and take off jewellery, and brush their hair. This style is typical: veneered in mahogany and with little drawers for keeping trinkets. The central drawer is lockable to keep safe precious letters, locks of hair and jewellery. Regency furniture has cachet at the moment, thus the guide price at auction was £300–£400/€350–465/$480–640.

Early 19th century giltwood mirror

This elegant mirror is typical of the Regency period with its nod to Neo-classical style in the use of columns and Doric capitals. The basic wood frame has been covered in smooth gesso then gilded, with moulded composite decoration added afterwards. Furniture businesses found it cheaper to employ a composite moulder than a skilled wood carver, so composite mirrors are widely found. Composite is hard and unyielding compared to wood, but is more affordable – this one fetched £350/€405/$560 at auction.

Victorian over-mantel mirror

This attractive giltwood mirror, c1860, would have been installed over a drawing room fireplace, giving a focal point to the room and enhancing light sources such as candle sconces and oil lamps – the electric light bulb was invented in the 1880s, but not widely installed until the 20th century. Measuring 1.5m/5ft tall and a little over 1m/3.3ft wide, the gilded wooden mirror frame has an 'archtop' design and achieved £200/€230/$320 at auction.

Late 19th century oval mirror

Plain oval mirrors such as these, with unadorned wooden frames, were popular at the end of the Victorian era. Made in mahogany with satinwood stringing (inlaid wood), such an understated piece would have enhanced the parlour or hallway of a middling household. Similar mirrors are widely available in antiques shops and at fairs and can be found for under £100/€115/$160.

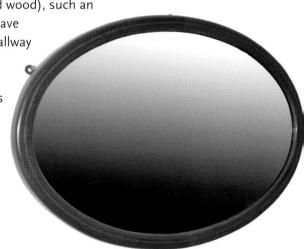

Storage

Cupboards, cabinets & shelves

We tend to think of storage as a late 20th century concept, but it's been a common preoccupation for much longer. If you visit an 18th or 19th century house with all its period features intact you'll find built-in china cupboards, book shelves, dressers and linen cupboards. Dedicated display cabinets became popular when ordinary folk started collecting ornaments and china tea sets 'for best' in the 19th century. Prices for antique storage can be very competitive, especially for old coffers and late Victorian and Edwardian bookcases, which can be snapped up for just a few hundred pounds/euros/dollars from a shop.

Early 19th century sideboard

Made in highly figured mahogany, this breakfront sideboard of 1825 is stamped with the 'Gillows' mark, indicating that it was made by Gillows of Lancaster, the renowned furniture makers who equipped many well-to-do houses in the north and the Midlands of England. 'Breakfront' means that the smooth line of the piece 'breaks' in the middle – outwards or inwards. The sideboard is a late 18th century invention for serving food and as Gillows pieces are very collectable, this piece went for £1,000/€1,150/$1,600 at auction.

Early 20th century display cabinet

Late Georgian style, particularly elegant Sheraton, was revived in the early 20th century, with the result that you can get the look without having to pay the astronomic price of an original – this display cabinet was £850/€990/$1,360 at auction. It is made from mahogany and kingwood and has 'astragal glazed' cabinet doors – glass panels that are divided up by glazing bars to create a decorative pattern. At nearly 2m/6.5ft high, it would make a capacious piece of storage for a study or living room.

French provincial cupboard

Vernacular country furniture can look very smart in modern settings, offering a chunky focal point to a room. This restored 18th century example is made from oak, and the old wood has an attractive striped grain. With long panelled or 'raised and fielded' doors, it would have been used to store household items such as linen. At 146cm/57.5in high and 54cm/21in deep it is ideal storage for a bedroom, kitchen or hall and cost £300/€350/$480 at auction.

French hanging cupboard

Made in around 1880, this cupboard is special, both for its richly coloured walnut wood veneer that has developed a good patina, and its pleasing shape, resulting in a guide price of £800–1,200/€930–1,400/$1,280–1,920 at auction. The carved decorative details on the panelled doors draw the eye to the beautiful grain of the old wood. Hanging furniture – including cupboards, corner cupboards and shelves – was popular in the 19th century and used space efficiently in households that were buying ever more china, glassware, ornaments and books. Much cheaper pieces of hanging furniture, often in pine, can be found at fairs and antiques centres.

Regency waterfall bookcase

Waterfall bookcases are so named because their shelves get deeper the further down the case they are, creating a waterfall effect. While some period bookcases are towering, due to the high ceilings of well-to-do houses of the time, this one is small, elegant and narrow. It incorporates a cupboard and has its original paint. Such practical Regency pieces are sought after, as this example illustrates with a £2,500/€2,900/$4,000 price tag at a fair, but there are much more affordable versions available from the late Victorian and Edwardian periods.

19th century deed rack

A Victorian deed rack transforms into an unusual yet versatile set of shelves today. These oak racks were once common in lawyers' offices, but have been replaced by high tech filing cabinets and digital storage. With five slatted tiers, the 2m/6.5ft high, 1.5m/5ft wide rack would suit a home office or a large kitchen. In good condition, this rack fetched £1,500/€1,740/$2,400 at auction, definitely the place to look for them.

Wardrobes & chests

In the 18th century clothes and household linen were stored in linen presses or clothes presses, known as *armoires* in France. They were large cupboards consisting of sliding trays, a shallow space for hanging clothes from pegs and a set of drawers. The wardrobe with a hanging rail developed in the 19th century and ranged from single door versions to double and triple doors – some late 19th century Arts & Crafts-style wardrobes are spectacular in width. Chests of drawers were also standard furniture for storing clothes and linen. Sometimes drawers are lined in a different kind of wood from the main body of the chest, such as oak or cedar, which is a sign of craftsmanship and quality. Late Victorian and Edwardian wardrobes and chests are particularly good value for money and can be found priced at several hundred and upwards.

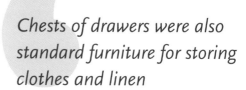

Chests of drawers were also standard furniture for storing clothes and linen

Regency linen press

Linen presses are a combination of drawers, and a short hanging space with pegs and shelves. Although made of mahogany, this 1815 version has faded over time, probably by sunlight, hence its guide price at auction of £400–£600/€465–700/$640–960. Period linen presses have often undergone adaptation in the 20th century, with extra shelves or new hanging rails added; and some antiques dealers sell linen presses that have been converted to all hanging space, by taking out drawers and shelves beneath. Whether converted or not, they make great spaces for storing bed and table linen, and clothes.

Victorian marquetry wardrobe

This is a good example of a large, late 19th century wardrobe, decorated with marquetry inlay. Made from mahogany, it is designed in the manner of Maple & Co, at the time one of the world's most successful furniture emporiums, based in London's Tottenham Court Road. The company made furniture for the home and the export market. This wardrobe came with an en-suite dressing table and the whole set cost £650/€755/$1,040 at auction.

Victorian dressing table

By the late 19th century a new piece of bedroom furniture became popular – the dressing table, which superseded the traditional dressing glass placed on a chest or small table. Consisting of drawers on each side and a swing mirror, this type of dressing table became the blueprint for those produced well into the 1960s. The 1880s Victorian version shown here is made from figured walnut and has a glamorous design that fetched £700/€810/$1,120 at auction.

Overlooked for many years, Victorian and Edwardian dressing tables (and later vintage examples, too) are great value today and can be found for considerably less than this.

Continental provincial armoire

Prettily carved doors and long brass lock escutcheons give femininity to an 18th century oak *armoire* that fetched £550/€638/$880 at auction. In Europe, *armoires* were often given to couples as celebrations of a marriage, and were kept in the hallway where they could be viewed and admired by visitors. Watch out for impressively sized *armoires* from Eastern Europe which are filtering through to antiques fairs at reasonable prices.

Late 18th century chest on chest

The chest on chest, or tallboy, was a standard piece of Georgian furniture. The two chests were placed one on top of another for ease of erection and transport; the top half always had two short drawers and three long drawers, while the bottom half had three deeper, long drawers.

This capacious mahogany example, standing on bracket feet, would have been used to store clothes and linen and has an original 'brushing slide' in the middle – a sliding shelf that pulls out so that clothes could be prepared for wear. Its guide price at auction was £500–£800/€580–930/$800–1,280.

Regency bowfront chest of drawers

In the 19th century, the chest on chest was overtaken in popularity by the single chest. Just over 1m/3.3ft high, 1m/3.3ft wide, and 50cm/20in deep, this mahogany bowfront chest, c1815, provides compact storage space for clothes and table linen. With the classic combo of two short and three long drawers, it sits on outswept bracket feet and sold for a competitive £240/€278/$385 at auction.

Victorian pine chest of drawers

In the 19th century, pine was used to make carcases for fine furniture veneered with more expensive rosewood, mahogany and walnut. It was also used to make workaday kitchen, bedroom and country-style furniture. A simple pine chest of drawers such as this probably would have been painted white or cream, but most of these pieces have now been stripped back to the original wood. A large chest of drawers such as this would cost around £600/€700/$960 in a shop.

Victorian collector's chest

Constructed from walnut in the late 19th century, this chest might have housed a keen naturalist's collection of butterflies, insects, birds' eggs or dried flowers. Collector's chests could be lined with velvet and/or the drawers compartmentalised to file collections in an orderly way. Now such a piece of furniture would make a noteworthy place for storing stationery, bills and household paperwork. This fetched £700/€810/$1,120 at auction.

19th century red lacquer chest

Attributed to the craftsmen of the Indonesian settlement of Batavia, now absorbed by the capital city of Jakarta, this striking red chest dates to around 1800. It is finished with layers of red lacquer and painted with Chinoiserie decoration depicting pagodas, timber pavilions, mountains and sea. Even the brass handles have an exotic flavour, with what seem to be little dragonheads curling upwards. Old, rare and unusual, a piece such as this commanded a price of over £4,000/€4,640/$6,400 at a fair.

Coffers

Coffers, also referred to as chests, have a long history and are one of the most enduring furniture designs. From medieval times they were used for storing important things, from linen and clothing to ledgers, documents, pewter and silver, jewels and money. Old examples can often be seen in churches today, for storing clerical vestments. They also doubled up as makeshift seats and tables. These days, coffers represent good value for antiques lovers, and 17th century examples can be bought at prices in the low hundreds at auction.

17th century oak coffer

It's incredible to think that this piece of oak furniture has been in circulation for over 300 years and is still going strong. A narrow 37cm/14.5in in depth, but just over 1m/3.3ft wide, this coffer has a decorative carved 'lunette' frieze on the front, which simply means that the carving sits in a semicircular field. Oak was the wood of choice for unsophisticated, country pieces such as this, which sold for £150/€175/$240 at auction.

17th century English panelled chest

At 120cm/47in wide and 50cm/20in deep, this oak coffer is bigger
and deeper than its cousin (opposite), and has far more elaborate
decorative carving, consisting of patera (floral motifs) within lozenges
and a lunette frieze. Dated to around 1660, it also has a more complex
structure made by a craftsman joiner, which ensured a price of
£650/€755/$1,040 at auction.

17th century English plank chest

Thought to date to 1620, this oak
coffer is of very simple
construction that would not have
required much skill to make, just
joining planks together with nails
and iron bands. It is comparatively
small at 83cm/33in wide and
36cm/14in deep, but with its
'trestle' feet has a prettiness about it that would suit a bedroom or
bathroom today. It fetched £600/€700/$960 at auction.

06

Talking point antiques

Talking point antiques

When buying antiques some styles of furniture have particularly interesting stories behind them that capture the imagination. Other pieces are a cut above the rest: investments that will stand the test of time and hold their value. The ten highlights that follow are interesting and intriguing for both reasons.

Arts & Crafts furniture

The Arts & Crafts movement began gaining momentum in Britain in the early 1860s when artist and designer William Morris and his associates rejected the overblown Victorian interior style of the time in favour of a simpler look that re-embraced craftsmanship and rejected the techniques of mass production. Morris himself was not a cabinet-maker but designed furnishing fabrics, wallpaper, tiles, stained glass, carpets and tapestries – original 'Morris & Co' wallpaper and fabric patterns are still available today under licence to Sanderson (www.william-morris.co.uk). Morris & Co also made fine furniture. As the 19th century progressed, the Arts & Crafts philosophy spread across the decorative arts and furniture design, influencing top furniture makers including the Barnsley Brothers (Ernest and Sidney) and their

associate Ernest Gimson who set up workshops in Sapperton, Gloucestershire. More affordable Arts & Crafts style designs were created by Sir Ambrose Heal for Heal & Son in London, and by other 'middling' furniture emporiums. In America the most renowned Arts & Crafts furniture maker was Gustav Stickley, whose pieces are highly sought after today and can be seen at the Stickley Museum at Craftsman Farms in New Jersey (www.stickleymuseum.org).

Arts & Crafts style furniture has a definite character, with methods of construction exposed to celebrate the craftsmanship and the honesty of the materials. So, mortise-and-tenon joints, dovetail joints and hinges and handles in finely wrought ironmongery are usually visible. Particular motifs were incorporated into carved panels, ironmongery and copper decorations, such as the heart, the trefoil (the outline of three overlapping circles, commonly seen in church windows), the tulip, the rose and other stylised flowers and leaves.

Wood of course was the major component of Arts & Crafts style furniture, especially traditional and durable oak, which was sometimes stained darker to give it a warm, antique feel, and to bring out the patterns in the grain.

Arts & Crafts furniture is light enough in colour to fit into most contemporary homes, as this Scottish Arts & Crafts bedroom suite, c1900, pages 120/121, shows. It comprises wardrobe, dressing table and washing stand with inlaid blue glass panels and copper roundels; simple yet elegant, the suite fetched £1,800/€2,100/$2,900 at auction. The stained pine hall settle, c1900, is decorated with roses; with neat proportions, it sold for £1,100/€1,300/$1,760 at auction.

The Windsor chair

An iconic English design, this comfortable armchair dates back to the early 18th century, according to the latest research by authorities Michael Harding-Hill and Robert Parrott. The first examples were probably made in or around Windsor, England, hence the name. The construction is simple, with 'stick' or 'spindle' legs inserted into the underside of the seat and a 'stick' backrest and arms inserted into the topside of the seat.

Windsor chairs were versatile – used in kitchens, parlours and libraries (the Bodleian Library in Oxford has some dating to 1756). They were used outdoors too, painted green to protect the wood and known as 'Forest Chairs'.

Native woods were used to make these portable yet solid chairs and, according to Ivan G Sparkes, former Curator of the Wycombe Chair Museum in Buckinghamshire, England, this typically meant elm

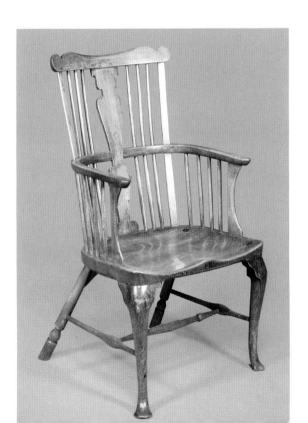

for the seat – which was always shaped like a saddle; beech for turned parts such as legs and the 'stretchers' that held the legs together and made the chair stronger; and ash, yew or fruitwood for the parts that needed to be bent using steam techniques – arms and back rails, and curving sticks for the backrest. In America, pine and poplar were used to make the seats, with oak, ash and hickory preferred for the turned and steam-bent parts.

Over the years the Windsor chair has had many guises, as an armchair, a side chair, a rocking chair, a settee, a low-back chair and a child's chair. And the styles are numerous too, from comb-backs to fan-backs, shawl-backs to balloon-backs, bow-backs to spindle-backs. Decorative 'splats' (the vertical member in the centre of a chairback) were often a feature. Some chairs have cabriole-shaped legs, others pad feet, all according to the fashion of the times.

By the 19th century the Windsor chair industry in England was centred in the Chilterns, Buckinghamshire, where millions of these chairs were produced using raw materials from the surrounding wooded landscape. It is estimated that around 4,500 Windsor chairs were made each day in the High Wycombe area to meet demand.

Today, some examples are highly collectable, particularly early 18th century chairs. At auction expect to pay £300–£400/€350–465/$480–640 for a 19th century Windsor chair, such as this simple example (left) with a hooped back and turned, tapering legs, to £700–£1,200/€810–1,400/$810–1,920 for a rarer example such as the late 18th century ash and elm high-back Windsor chair (page 123) with cabriole legs. At antiques shops they can be bought from around £300/€350/$480 each.

Regency chaise longue

The British Regency period was an era of flamboyance, when fine furniture makers were influenced not only by Neo-classical style, but also Egyptian style, Gothic style and Oriental Chinoiserie. The most elegant of these modes was the Neo-classical, which emphasised symmetry and a lightness of design based on the clean lines and strong shapes seen in ancient Greek and Roman architecture and artefacts. Popular decorative motifs included the Greek key pattern, classical urn shapes, garlands, lion masks and lion paws (look out too for scarabs, sphinxes and hieroglyphics inspired by Egyptian history). In America the similar style and period is referred to as Federal, and in France as Empire.

In furniture terms, the Regency period spans the decades from 1800 to 1830 and is so named because George, then Prince of Wales (later the Prince Regent, and later still, King George IV), was a style-setter who loved opulent decor. Sparing no expense, he remodelled

Windsor Castle, and created a lavish residence at Carlton House in St James's, London (demolished in 1825), and another at the Royal Pavilion in Brighton on the Sussex coast (which is open to the public today).

The more restrained style of Regency furniture looks good in modern interiors because of its simplicity and understated elegance. This chaise longue has a visible show-wood frame made in expensive rosewood with brass inlay – a typical Regency feature, along with brass castors that made it easy to move furniture around. Its design is based on the French *méridienne* style of chaise longue, with a higher headrest connected to a lower footrest with a sloping side. New upholstery in a fine fabric makes this a very desirable piece of furniture, with a price tag of £4,500/€5,200/$7,200 at a fair.

Thonet bentwood furniture

Michael Thonet (pronounced 'Tonet' with a hard initial 't'), a joiner born in Prussia in 1796, created one of the most recognisable styles of the 19th century: bentwood furniture. He experimented for many years with bending wood in iron clamps using the heat of steam and, by 1859, the technique had been patented and his 'Chair No 14', formed of steam-bent solid beech, was ready to go into mass production. It is still produced today as 'Chair No 214'.

The lightweight chair was fixed together with screws so it could be simply assembled; in fact, 36 disassembled chairs could fit into a cubic metre box, making them easy and cheap to export. The 'Chair No 14' design has later been referred to as both the 'Vienna coffee house chair' and as the 'Consumer chair', and was sold to bistros, bars and restaurants all over Europe and America.

The company, by then known as Gebrüder Thonet (Thonet Brothers), set up in London and New York as well as Vienna. 'Rocking chair No 1' was launched in 1860, followed by later models with different designs of twirling bentwood. The bentwood range grew to include deckchairs, bar stools, folding theatre stools, settees and hat stands. Thonet's patent on the technique expired in 1869 so there are many lookalikes out there, but originals have stamped or paper marks on the seat frame or underneath the chair. In addition, all models were recorded in Thonet catalogues.

Thonet furnishings are classic heirloom pieces and may well be inherited rather than found in any great quantity in antiques shops – expect to pay between £300–£600/€350–700/$480–770 for a basic rocking chair in reasonable condition (below). The Thonet company remains family-owned, and is based in Germany, where it offers to authenticate antique Thonet furniture if supplied with clear photographic evidence. To carry out research go to www.thonet.de.

Biedermeier furniture

As with Arts & Crafts furniture, Biedermeier is a style rather than the work of a single maker. The form evolved in the first half of the 19th century across Germany, Austria, Russia, Scandinavia and other northern European countries as an alternative to the rather grand Empire style. Homely-looking Biedermeier furniture was aimed at comfortable 'middling' households and the generic name refers to the conservative families who bought it.

All sorts of woods were used to make Biedermeier furniture,

depending on what was available locally, but showing the grain off was important, and pieces were simply planed and polished. Timbers ranged from rich-toned mahogany, walnut and beech, to lighter ash, birch, poplar and elm – the paler woods were popular in the Scandinavian countries and Russia. Details such as inlaid strips of a darker wood, known as 'cross-banding', were used to subtly frame a piece, while shapes of feet and legs varied widely from maker to maker, country to country. All Biedermeier furniture has in common a generous, rounded look, which is simply ornamented or decoratively carved if at all.

All Biedermeier furniture has in common a generous, rounded look, which is simply ornamented or decoratively carved if at all

The beauty of Biedermeier antiques is that there is much to choose from, as these fair buys show. The two matching Biedermeier-style bedside tables pictured are made from birch; they date to around 1880 and were priced at £2,400/€2,800/$3,840 for the pair. The Empire-style sofa, £3,500/€4,100/$5,600, is made of silver birch. The Biedermeier armchair, probably from a set of dining chairs, earlier, dating to around 1830 and constructed from cherry wood; the arching swan necks are a wonderful flourish, hence the price of £3,400/€3,950/$5,440 for pair (one shown left).

Longcase clocks

The longcase clock evolved from the 17th century, and comprised a tall wooden case in oak, walnut or mahogany, a movement, a pendulum that improved accuracy, and a highly visible clock face framed by a removable hood with carved decoration. At the beginning of the 18th century it became fashionable to include a glazed window called a 'lenticle' in the body of the clock, behind which the bob of the pendulum could be seen swinging.

In the 18th and 19th centuries many longcase clocks – affectionately known as grandfather clocks – were made. They had eight-day or one-day (30-hour) movements, before needing to be re-wound; some also had moon-phase dials to show the age of the moon. Commonly they struck a bell on the hour.

Grandfather clocks can be anything from 1.8m/6ft up to 2.4m/8ft tall and are imposing pieces of furniture. Smaller grandmother and granddaughter clocks were also made. These ranged in size from 1.2m/4ft to 1.8m/6ft tall to fit into less spacious rooms with lower ceilings.

The Swedish Mora clock is a variation of the longcase clock, with an eight-day movement. These curvaceous clocks were made from the late 18th century in and around a town called Mora in the Dalarna region of Sweden. Making Mora clocks was very much a cottage industry and local families specialised in making one part: dials, movements, pendulums or cases, for example. The wooden cases were painted white, cream or pale grey or blue – the colours of the Gustavian palette, which reflected light in the dark winter months and was influenced by the French fashion for pale colours too. Sometimes the cases and faces were hand painted with flowers and leaves.

While they are looming, longcase clocks make a great statement in a hall or living room and have a reassuring, deep, tick-tock. They can be found for as little as £1,000/€1,160/$1,600 in a shop, depending on condition. The Victorian example pictured, in mahogany, fetched £1,400/€1,625/$2,240 at auction.

Antique desks

From the early 18th century onwards, as furniture designs for specific activities flourished, so designs for desks and bureaux proliferated. Correspondence was a popular pastime as well as essential for business. Among the range were dainty desks for women known as *bonheur du jour*, the more masculine *bureau à gradin* with tiered drawers on top of the writing surface, and cleverly designed tambour desks with a protective roll-down front. Most of them had shallow drawers for keeping quills, ink and sealing wax, and small compartments for paper.

It is thought that the Carlton House style of desk (top right) is so named because it was designed for the Prince of Wales for his magnificent mansion, Carlton House in St James's, his London

18th century mahogany bureau

residence from 1783. The desk is characterised by having several tiers of drawers ranged in a U-shape, known as a 'curved gallery', above the surface of the desk, and a leather-covered writing area. They continued to be produced throughout the 19th century, and remain a popular style today, although top quality examples can be pricey, around or over £5,000/€5,800/$8,000.

The French *bureau plat* or writing table (bottom right) has a simple long top and shallow drawers underneath. The 19th century example shown here has been ebonised, or stained black to resemble expensive ebony. It also has a leather inlay for writing upon. A *bureau plat* in good condition will be between £2,000–£3,000/€2,300–€3,500/$3,200–4,800 at a fair.

Ultimate armchairs

In the days when open fires heated houses and draughts eddied through window frames, doors and floorboards, seating was designed to cocoon the body as much as possible. The upholstered wing armchair kept the sitter snug from draughts, and shielded the face from the heat of the fire.

Early 18th century wing chairs in good condition are very sought after; however, as with much antique furniture, later versions are more

affordable. The late 18th century version pictured was priced at under £2,000/€2,300/$3,200 at a fair.

The generously proportioned *bergère* chair was a French furniture staple. It does not have a high back as the traditional wing chair does, but envelops the body with a solid back and closed, rather than open, arms as the *fauteuil* does. This example below dates to the early 19th century and has been reupholstered. The paint on the beechwood frame is original, making the chair very desirable and able to command a price of £4,500/€5,200/$7,200 at a fair.

Campaign furniture

Campaign furniture developed as a practical response to the many wars fought during the 19th century. Increasingly army officers required portable furniture that echoed life back home. As well as demand from soldiers, the hundreds of thousands of military and civilian staff sent out to all corners of the British Empire also fuelled the market for furniture that was easy to transport by cart and camel.

Campaign furniture was cleverly made with screws and detachable joints so that it could be dismantled and packed into custom-made storage boxes with the minimum of fuss. Sofas could be broken down into parts – legs, seat, arms; chairs folded up; table stems had telescopic columns; and bookcase doors and shelves could be lifted off. Handles were set into furniture to give a flat front, and brass bands were inlaid into the vulnerable corner edges to avoid damage from knocks and scrapes.

Pieces could be ingeniously metamorphic too: a chair that could serve as a single bed; a chest of drawers that slid apart in the middle and became a desk; a bidet that turned into a stool. The range of campaign furniture was huge, from armchairs and dining chairs to beds, chests of drawers, large dining tables and even four-tiered whatnots. Each piece unscrewed or lifted apart, which led to it becoming known as 'knockdown' furniture.

The early 19th century campaign chest with protective brass banding, pictured, is a classic example. It would have had a sturdy lock to keep valuables safe – the interior would have been fitted with drawers. Placed on a stand with casters to raise it up off the floor, it could be used as an occasional table too. Highly collectable, a piece such as this would be around or over £5,000/€5,800/$8,000 at a fair or shop. This elegant settee, c1860, with cane arms, seat and back, swiftly comes apart with a few twiddles of the brass catches, and at £3,800/€4,400/$6,100 is more affordable. Not everything in the campaign stable is as expensive, so keep your eyes open if it's an area that interests you.

Dressers

Dressers have been popular for over three centuries to store and display cooking pots, kitchen utensils, china and ornaments. With utility and affordability in mind, they were made from readily available local wood such as pine and oak. In Wales the dresser became something of an art form during the 18th and 19th centuries, and a treasured heirloom that was passed down through the family, according to Welsh furniture expert Richard Bebb of Welsh Antiques (www.welshantiques.com). Rather than being viewed as a piece of kitchen furniture, the Welsh dresser, called a china hutch in the US, was placed in the principal living room of a house to display the best china and ornaments. Even small cottages were furnished with comparatively large dressers.

Today, the best 18th century Welsh dressers cost upwards of £15,000/€17,400/$24,000, but later 19th century examples are available for under £4,000/€4,640/$6,400. The older dressers tend to have open plate racks, whereas the later ones are enclosed; some have an empty space in the middle known as the 'dog kennel' where pets can sleep.

Plain pine dressers from the 18th and 19th centuries often come up at auction and antiques fairs – a basic late 19th century dresser in reasonable condition could set you back £1,000/€1,160/$1,600 at a fair, or an older late Georgian example in need of some restoration, such as the one pictured, several thousand pounds/euros/dollars at auction.

With utility and affordability in mind, they were made from readily available local wood such as pine and oak

07

Reinvention

Reinvention

There was such a wide variety of furniture made in the 19th and early 20th centuries that sometimes we wonder how to use it today. What to do with a tiered whatnot, for example, or a glass-topped *bijouterie* (a display case for small silver pieces and/or jewellery), or a rustic dough bin, or a sideboard? Many of these pieces have good storage and display potential, and of course can be used in any room of the home, not just the one they were intended for.

Think smart

A whatnot could house cookery books, while a *bijouterie* could become a display cabinet for family keepsakes and mementoes. A dough bin is just crying out to be filled with linen, towels, or toys, and a sideboard certainly doesn't have to live in a dining room: it could as easily be adapted for use in a bedroom, study or hall. In a similar vein, a dresser can come out of the kitchen – and be used in the study for keeping books, folders and papers; a pair of industrial bellows could become an unusual coffee table, stacked up on some columns of hardback books if you've got nothing else to hand. A Victorian plant

stand makes a great lamp table, and a 19th century collector's chest is perfect for storing CDs, DVDs and household bric-à-brac. The trick is not to be hidebound by what has gone before, but to think about antiques in a way that suits the way you live today.

Dough bins are a remnant of another age when bakers proved bread dough in large wooden bins. The one pictured is made of oak, but elm was also used. At nearly a metre wide and half a metre deep it would make a fantastic and quirky storage piece today, ideal for use in a kitchen or utility room, or in a bedroom for storing linen and blankets

BUYER'S TIP: *TAKE A MODERN VIEW*

When browsing antique furniture, think about the piece in terms of what it offers now. Look for storage and shelving opportunities, and space-saving furniture that can be tucked away, such as whatnots, plant stands, tilt-top tables and nests of occasional tables. If inexpensive antique furniture appears dark and looming, imagine how it would look painted a pale, muted colour – painting could make all the difference to how a piece fits in with your other furniture.

A pair of giant mid-19th century industrial bellows made of elm and leather could be transformed into a stunning coffee table top

Their hygienic tiled tops and sturdy pitch pine legs mark out these late 19th century tables as dairy furniture. Now they would make a lovely pair of kitchen tables for preparing food or dining

The trick is not to be hidebound by what has gone before, but to think about antiques in a way that suits the way you live today

Tiered shelves known as whatnots abounded in the 19th century, and were a standard piece of furniture in parlours and drawing rooms. They were used for holding ornamental knick-knacks, books and miscellanea. They come in square shapes, or triangular to fit into corners – and are just as space-saving today.

Reupholstering antique seating

Hailing from Provence in the South of France, this 19th century walnut three-seater bench has had its seat pad reupholstered in rustic-style check linen.

There is a glut of 19th century sofas, chaises longues and chairs available from shops and at auction, often with attractive show-wood walnut and rosewood frames (where the wooden frame is visible and a decorative feature). However, many of them have worn-out fabric and stuffing and springs that need replacing. Upholstery is a skilled craft so, unless you have been taught how, it's best to employ a professional to do the reupholstering work for you. What you'll get in return is a chic item that looks as up to date or as period as you want it to, depending on your choice of fabric. Some upholsterers keep a stock of reupholstered or ready-to-reupholster furniture, in which case you can choose the fabric. Stripes are Regency in style, floral patterns and plain velvets are mid- to late Victorian in look, while a plain, vivid shade of fabric or an outsize pattern have a contemporary twist.

With regard to the stuffing, pay for the best you can afford. The most expensive is horsehair which is usually reserved for conservation projects; a more affordable option, popular with upholsterers, is pure animal hair (hog and cattle mix); even less expensive is animal hair carded together with synthetic black fibre. If new coil springs are required it may be advisable to opt for a size smaller than the originals as modern springs are very strong in comparison.

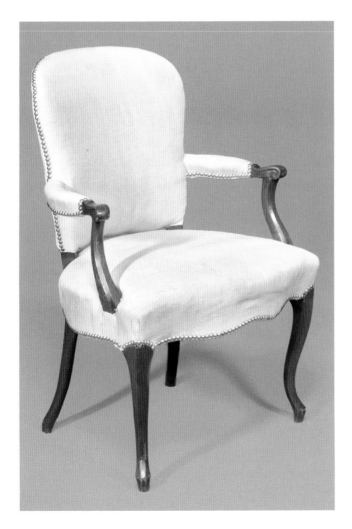

This pretty 'open elbow' armchair in the French style has elegant cabriole legs. With the back, seat and arms newly stuffed and re-upholstered in white linen, finished with brass studs, it has taken on a contemporary feel

A 19th century sofa has been re-upholstered and covered in turquoise velvet, and the gilded frame restored. Petite, yet deep, this piece has lovely proportions and would fit well in a smaller room

Painting furniture

At auction and in antiques shops you will find plenty of unremarkable dark wood furniture with low price tags to match – cupboards and benches, chests of drawers, wardrobes, shelves, tables and old church furniture that may have a bit of damage too, a split in the wood, or a poor finish. Don't dismiss them out of hand because, with a coat or two of satin finish paint, these pieces could be transformed.

Before painting you'll need to clean the wood of the layers of built-up dirt and polish with a solution of sugar soap mixed with warm water – wring out the cloth before you apply it to the wood so as not to soak and raise the grain, and wear protective gloves. Allow the surface to dry fully before rubbing down with a fine sandpaper to create a key for the paint – wipe away any debris with a clean cloth. When thoroughly dry, apply an undercoat of acrylic primer, let it dry for the recommended number of hours, then paint over a coat of acrylic satin finish (or eggshell) in your desired colour – pale, muted tones seem to work well. If you prefer a slightly distressed finish, rub over a few patches on the edges with fine sandpaper to give a timeworn look.

If you prefer a limed finish, preferably choose a piece of

furniture that is made of a hardwood such as oak, ash or mahogany, with an open grain (pine is a softwood and has a smoother grain, so liming is less effective). For best results buy a preparatory liming kit from a specialist company such as Liberon. Use a bronze stiff-wired brush to gently open up the grain, then wipe clean with a tack cloth (a cloth coated with resin to pick up dust). Then start to work in the liming wax by hand using fine steel wool, wiping up any residue as you go. Buff up using a neutral wax paste.

 NEED TO KNOW: *PALE AND INTERESTING*

There is a trend among some dealers to bleach dark wood furniture to a paler finish to suit the modern preference for lighter coloured wood and make large items such as unremarkable marquetry cabinets and *armoires* more saleable. There is a precedent – in the 19th century paler woods were regularly stained darker to resemble more expensive timbers such as mahogany, walnut and rosewood. It would not be advisable to bleach a high quality antique as this would reduce its value.

The confident, even strident, design of this 1830 French mahogany 'show-wood' frame sofa is toned down with a pale grey striped fabric

View furniture as a foil

The dominant taste in new furniture over the last decade has been for blond woods, but with the return of richer walnut to the scene, dark woods are creeping back into consideration. In fact the rich brown tones of woods such as walnut, dark stained oak, mahogany and rosewood look classic and beautiful set against bold fabric and wallpaper patterns and the vibrant paint colours that are so fashionable today. Antique furniture can be the thread that draws a room together, adding a calming, familiar note to an adventurous decorating scheme.

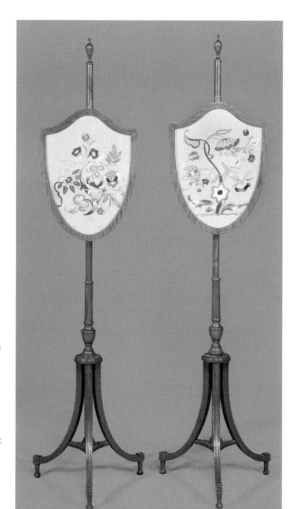

Polescreens were common in the days of the open fire and were designed to protect women's faces from the heat of the flames. This satinwood pair, dating to 1900, would make a quirky talking point in a sitting room

A long window seat from the Regency period has been reupholstered in cream linen. With scrolled ends, this is every inch the elegant addition to a bedroom or living room

 HOT BUY: *CHURCH FURNITURE*

Ever thought of bringing a pew into your home? Former church furniture can be extremely good value, both in terms of price and quality. As churches refurbish with new furniture there is a steady flow of antique pews, throne chairs, side chairs, tables and bookcases on sale in antiques shops and at salvage yards. A spate of church building in the late 19th and early 20th centuries means that there is plenty of Victorian and Edwardian furniture available, much of it made from solid oak or pine – congregations bought the best they could afford – and now costing in the low hundreds of pounds, euros or dollars. Pews can be cut down to suit your space, and/or painted for a more contemporary look – they make great hall benches, or seating for dining and sitting areas. Other items such as collection dishes and lecterns are easily reinvented into quirky key bowls and cookbook stands.

08

Caring for your investment

Caring for your investment

So, you've brought home your antique find or beloved heirloom, and shifted it into place. Now what? Just like any piece of furniture, treat it well and it will look good for many years to come. Like all natural materials wood is subject to environmental conditions, so consider where to place your piece to lessen any potential problems.

Taking care

First, bright sunshine can alter the colour of wood – dark wood may fade, conversely pale wood may darken, so use blinds and curtains to provide shade. Secondly, wood doesn't like direct heat, so place furniture away from radiators, stoves and open fires to prevent the timber from drying out, splitting, or joints shrinking and loosening. When turning the heating on for winter do it steadily and slowly, rather than creating a dramatic change in air temperature, to acclimatise the wood.

In a very humid atmosphere wood can develop patches of bloom, a whitish mould that smells musty; the best way of preventing this is by encouraging good air circulation in a room (open a window daily to draw in fresh air) and around the furniture – don't push it

flush against the wall, leave a little gap so the air can flow, and open drawers and doors regularly. In very hot climates, a de-humidifier will help remove excess moisture from the air.

Handle with care

Antique furniture has stood the test of time, but that doesn't mean you can throw it around. Move pieces carefully and without putting too much strain on the joints and stress points such as legs. Generally speaking, a larger piece of furniture will need two people to lift it into position; dragging it may cause damage. A really heavy piece may need a person at each corner and webbing slings placed underneath the piece to be safely moved – wear stout shoes and gardening gloves to protect feet and hands.

If the furniture has doors, secure them with a piece of string before moving so that they can't flap open and damage the hinges or get knocked. Try not to lift chairs by their arms or back rails; place your hands underneath either side of the seat instead. If you have wooden floors in your living room or hall, consider putting fabric 'sliders' or pads on the bottom of furniture feet so that pieces can be moved easily across the floor without scratching it when you're cleaning.

Spotting insect attack

Woodworm is not a worm as such, but a beetle that lays its eggs in the crevices and corners of wood. It is the resulting larvae that tunnel into the wood and munch their way through it, leaving telltale 'woodworm' holes, before pupating and flying away to start the life

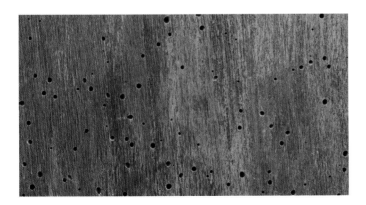

cycle again. Walnut and beech woods are more susceptible to the problem than mahogany and teak, but if you buy your furniture from a reputable dealer it is very unlikely to have woodworm in the first place. If woodworm is active you may see crisp, newly bored flight holes, and near them a little pile of 'frass' which looks like sawdust; old flight holes darken with age and lose the crispness of outline. If you think your item of furniture has got woodworm, contact a conservator for a second opinion and possible treatment with insecticide – a specialist job.

Buffing and polishing

All antique furniture benefits from regular dusting and buffing using a soft, dry tack cloth or lint-free duster that won't snag on raised areas of wood. Polish furniture two or three times a year, avoiding preparations containing silicone that produce an unnatural high shine. Opt instead for a natural beeswax polish and/or carnuba paste or liquid wax. Apply the wax sparingly with a clean cloth or duster, leave for a few minutes to harden a little then use elbow grease to buff up to a sheen. For carved wood, apply the wax sparingly with a soft bristle brush, then buff with a clean brush or cloth.

 BE INSPIRED: *EXPERT ADVICE*

For further in-depth information about caring for and repairing furniture of all kinds, check out:

Books
*Looking After Antiques by Frances Halahan and Anna Plowden (National Trust). This is an expert resource, covering everything from furniture to ceramics and glass.
*The National Trust Manual of Housekeeping (Elsevier). Details on how National Trust experts clean and maintain the collections held within the Trust's houses.
*Repairing & Restoring Chests & Cabinets by William Cook (Southwater). A step-by-step, project-based book for the amateur antique restorer.

Products
*Liberon specialise in products and kits specifically for the repair, care and re-finishing of wood furniture, including natural wax pastes, leather cream, retouch crayons, and a revival kit to rid furniture of wax build-up and heat or water rings (01797 367555; liberon.com).
*W S Jenkins specialise in products for wood, including polish, stains, varnish, metallic powders and bleach (020 8808 2336; wsjenkins.co.uk).
*Preservation Equipment Ltd offers a huge range of conservation grade cleaning products, cloths, brushes and tools (01379 647400; preservationequipment.com).
*Conservation Resources offers similar products to American customers (800 634 6932; conservationresources.com).

Professional help

If a quality antique is in need of expert first-aid – for example, if it has a damaged surface, unsightly cracks, an ugly varnish finish, flaking paint or gilding, worn wood stain, or is literally about to fall apart – it is best to take it to a professional restorer to repair. Such experts revive antiques in the most sympathetic way possible, using traditional methods.

It is also perfectly feasible to commission a professional to restore and replace cane and rush seating, and to reupholster chairs and sofas, though factor in this cost before purchasing an item. Original leather on chairs and desks is highly prized, as is original paint on furniture, so seek professional advice before attempting any restoration or removal. Things you can do yourself include buffing up leather with a proprietary leather cream, and touching up tiny areas of scratched wood with a touch-up pen.

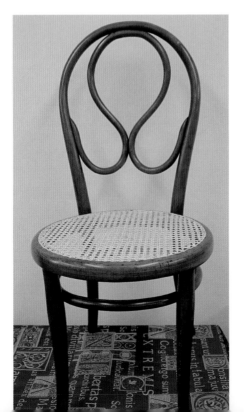

 NEED TO KNOW: *RESTORATION SPECIALISTS*

If you're looking for a restorer, start your search with a professional association. The British Antique Furniture Restorers' Association (BAFRA) represents craftsmen and women with at least five years' professional experience in the field (01935 83213; bafra.org.uk). The Institute of Conservation has a listing of qualified restorers in the UK and Ireland (020 3142 6799; conservationregister.com). The American Institute for Conservation of Historic and Artistic Works (AIC) holds details on conservators across the US (202 452 9545; conservation-us.org). There are similar organisations in most countries.

 INSTANT EXPERT: *QUICK FIXES*

- **Sticking drawers:** rub a plain white household candle along the runners of the drawer to make them slide more easily.
- **Removing white bloom:** brush it away with a soft-bristled brush then vacuum the area with a nozzle to capture any mould spores. Wipe over with a clean, damp cloth.
- **Spilt candle wax:** allow wax to harden and become brittle then scrape off with your thumbnail.
- **Minor wood repair:** scrape away old adhesive, then re-attach piece with a small amount of Scotch glue, wiping away any excess. Clamp in place or put a weight on top to consolidate gluing action and leave for 24 hours to set.
- **Cleaning away dirt:** use a small amount of conservation-grade detergent such as Vulpex diluted in water applied with a barely damp soft cloth, rinsed out frequently in clean water (do not get furniture wet or the wood grain will rise). Lightly pat down with a clean, damp cloth and allow to dry naturally over time. Do not wet metal elements such as handles, hinges or locks as they may rust.

09

Collectors

Bengt Lindvall and Lennart Svensson

01

Bengt Lindvall and Lennart Svensson first discovered the hilly, wooded countryside of mid-Scåne in Sweden in 1987, when they bought a run-down cottage to escape city life in Malmö at weekends. Within two years they had fallen sufficiently in love with the peaceful location and the late 16th century house – reputedly the oldest in the village of Billinge – to permanently relocate.

'This is such a friendly house, so inviting. I think the spirits of previous residents are grateful for what we've done,' says Bengt, wryly. And there has been much hard work involved – he and Lennart spent many hours renovating, decorating and sourcing furnishings, and in latter years have created an abundant cottage garden, dotted with antique ornaments and statuary and old tools.

Indoors, too, antiques are a major element in room schemes filled with pieces that are inherited, found at fairs and shops, and at flea markets and auctions. Both men grew up with antique furniture in their family homes and have always loved it. 'You inherit your eye,' explains Bengt of their taste for the old. 'My daughter Ulrica also has it! In fact, she's just re-homed a longcase clock that I inherited. It was made by the clockmaker Olof Keding of Landskrona, around 1800, and belonged to my great-grandfather.'

That's not to say that items from Ikea and other home stores don't creep in from time to time. 'Our philosophy is to mix things – we do not want to live in a museum so we add in a modern lamp or buy modern art for the walls, and oriental rugs. But we prefer old furniture, as long as it is usable, practical and not too expensive or pompous. We want to feel at ease.'

One of Bengt's favourite pieces of furniture is a long Gustavian sofa, dating to around 1780, which they bought from friends and dealers, Stenhuset Antikhandel in Stockamöllan, Scåne. 'It had been painted white so we gently stripped it using a knife, to get down to the original grey paint.' Restored and gorgeous, the sofa resides on the verandah, providing a comfy perch for taking tea. 'During winter we sit here with our Jack Russell dog, Lukas, and we also have dinner

parties on the verandah, seating up to ten guests around an English Victorian oak gateleg table. An old Swedish chandelier of the 1820s adds to the lovely atmosphere,' says Bengt.

In the kitchen they have a tall, antique Swedish stove, known as a *kakelungn*, constructed of glazed white bricks. 'We exchanged it for a clock with a chap who maintains *kakelungnar*,' recalls Bengt. 'In the winter we make fires in it every day, the smoke warms the whole stove which then radiates heat and keeps the kitchen warm.'

Also in the kitchen is an antique table for preparing food upon, and above it one of several early 19th century Swedish plate racks. 'We store our big plates in it: a mix of French faience above and painted plates from Scåne below. And we use them all, they are not just for show.'

Bengt and Lennart prefer painted furniture, in the Swedish tradition. 'In times past people couldn't afford mahogany and walnut so we had pine furniture, painted, and oak furniture that was left unpainted. The pine was painted in pale colours influenced by French fashions of the day, and which hid knots in the wood.' A creamy white buffet cabinet in the bathroom is a case in point, along with a pretty demi-lune pine table in a hallway. 'Even in the many fine houses and castles of the region, pine would have been commonplace,' comments Bengt.

Their philosophy of mixing old and new has spread to their most recent project, the renovation of the 19th century cottage next door, Lilla Råkeholm (lillarokeholm.se), which came up for sale a few years ago. 'We restored and redecorated it, and furnished it with lots of family pieces and items bought at auction. Now it is open all year as a bed and breakfast.'

Guests are invited to use the summerhouse – the result of another of Bengt and Lennart's 'lightbulb' moments. 'We collect things not knowing what to do with them. An acquaintance offered us some windows and doors salvaged from an old conservatory at nearby Rönneholm Castle. We bought a number of them then had an architect friend draw up a plan for a high-ceilinged, octagonal gazebo. People love to sit there with a glass of wine in the evening, with candlelight reflected in the old rippled glass.'

Both men relish the environment they've created from scratch over the years. Bengt concludes: 'Our style is very personal to us, a mix of old and new, functional and decorative, but we use everything. If you have Chinese porcelain, or silver cutlery, or antique furniture, use it. That makes for a friendly home.'

Sarah Florence Saumarez

02

Even on wintry days the elegant Georgian houses of Bath's famous crescents have a mellow glow thanks to the locally quarried limestone used to build them. Designer Sarah Florence Saumarez is lucky enough to live in one of these grand 18th century houses, in a small courtyard apartment. 'Externally the houses are preserved in almost perfect uniformity, but internally the townhouses vary a great deal. There are only a few original features remaining in my flat, such as window shutters and stone wine shelves,' she comments, a little ruefully.

Since moving here in 2009, this relatively blank canvas has given Florence an opportunity to develop her own style in the home that she shares with her two young sons. The décor is simple: floors of bare reclaimed timber beams that were sawn up to make floorboards, and

walls painted in Farrow & Ball's 'Skimming Stone' in the open-plan living area and richer 'Charleston Gray' in the main bedroom. There are elements of surprise too: small spaces are painted in dark, cosy colours and contain large-scale furniture. Under the dining room table she has painted a 'rug' on to the floorboards.

In the kitchen, monolithic concrete worktops and a large French marble pestle contrast with delicate pressed glass plates and Victorian Mochaware. It is a functional aesthetic, not at odds with the Georgian surroundings or present-day family living. In the sitting room a Swedish 1970s Parrot hanging chair, bought on eBay, swings happily next to an old sofa that Florence found at the local tip and had recovered with thick, slubby linen. In the boys' bedroom a pretty Georgian washstand stores Lego figures and small toys.

She explains: 'I like a look that's well lived in rather than immaculate, and antiques lend a sense of depth and history – such pieces have a patina that can only be achieved over time. Antique furniture goes with everything and, like old buildings, is very adaptable – I can always find a use for it. Because of my own interest and my interior design business, Florence & Co (www.florenceandcompany. com) I'm always looking in antiques shops and salvage yards. I prefer hunting in places that are a bit scruffy and making my own discoveries.'

She learned to love antiques early on in life, under her parents' influence. 'My mother adores antiques – she prefers polishing over cooking! Growing up, we lived among beautiful things, which instilled in me an appreciation and also an instinct to recognise pieces with honesty.' Florence's own collection started with an early 18th century Queen Anne writing bureau that belonged to her mother. She comments: 'My favourite style of furniture is from the Georgian period: there was great restraint in the way they designed which appeals to the modern eye.'

She's always adored the writing bureau and now it lives in the dining area and is used for storing stationery, ribbons and candles, while each of the boys has a narrow drawer in which to keep their special paintings and drawings. Nearby is a 17th century oak 'cricket table' (so called because the three legs are reminiscent of cricket

stumps) that was given to her by her aunt. 'For years it had a huge television on it and it was hard to appreciate. Now the top is a little split but I quite like the fact that it is not perfect.'

Florence appreciates an old oak coffer of a similar date for its original details: iron split hinges and a built-in box for holding candles and tapers. Now it is used to store fabrics awaiting projects. By her bedside is a Georgian bedside stand – a tiny cupboard on legs made from mahogany – and in an old writing slope she keeps a collection

of buttons. 'Lots of people have memories of playing with the treasures inside their mother's button boxes and I expect my little boys will do too!'

'I am always striving to refine my own taste,' she continues, 'and being able to edit is an important part of that. Too much clutter detracts from the beauty of the things but equally I'm not keen on a minimal environment. It is a question of finding a balance between the two – allowing special pieces breathing space but also having an abundance of things you love, adding layers of richness and interest to a room. Everything here is chosen for aesthetic and functional reasons and for being affordable. I'm afraid that being eco-friendly is simply a happy coincidence.'

Just as she grew up surrounded by antiques, Florence wants her children to appreciate them too and hankers after several more pieces for her ever-evolving home. 'I'd love a huge antique housekeeper's cupboard or perhaps museum cabinets to go along one wall. And I'd be quite happy if the cabinets came complete with a few ancient artefacts,' she says.

Robert McNellis

03

For most of his life Robert McNellis has lived in a Queen Anne-style house in the conservation area of Angelino Heights, one of Los Angeles' oldest suburbs, developed in the 1880s. The striking property, designated a historic monument, has overhanging eaves, a turret and three glorious wraparound porches. 'The neighbourhood is often used as a location in movies and has the largest concentration of 19th century Victorian and Queen Anne homes in southern California,' explains Robert.

It was his canny father, a policeman in the Los Angeles Police Department, who first bought the house where Robert grew up, then returned to as an adult 20 years ago. It was his father, too, who introduced him to the world of auctions and antiques at the tender age of 12.

'I tagged along with my father to the twice yearly LAPD's

unclaimed property auction – that's where I bought my first bike. My father frequently went to estate and antique sales too, where he bought paintings, Victorian lighting, and small collectables such as porcelain and art glass pieces by Lalique and Baccarat. I found that I loved going to auctions – the Sunday paper would list around 30 a week and I'd pick out a few and go.'

In adult life Robert has made a business out of his hobby. He deals in antique and vintage furniture and decorative objects, which he restores, and often repurposes, attending fairs and markets every month (for dates see www.robertsvintage.com). 'Having antiques in your home demonstrates a passion for visual interest and adds unique style,' he comments. 'These kinds of things are not pieces that you can buy at a furniture store or mall – they're one of a kind. Often antiques can be a good investment because certain things, such as pre-1860s furniture, were mostly made by hand.'

Additionally, Robert points out that much of the solid wood that American furniture was made of is no longer available. 'Tiger maple, quarter sawn oak, and American walnut and cherry trees were over-harvested and they're not available for furniture making any more. Many of the fittings on furniture from this era, such as hinges, locks and cabinet hardware, were made by hand too and were often marked by the maker.'

His Queen Anne home, which he is currently renovating, is a living reflection of Robert's furnishing philosophy. 'For my own home I'm looking for a less-is-more effect – interesting things, but not too many pieces. They have to be items that I can really live with and use. The fun thing about collecting is that I can indulge my moods and change things around when style trends evolve.'

Take his treasured solid walnut book-keeper's desk made in the mid 19th century, which naturally becomes the focal point of any room it's put in. 'It's a very clean, two-piece design and has lots of storage features. I'm moving things around because I'm renovating, but right now it's in my office, the former breakfast room of the house. The light that floods in from three big windows sets it off beautifully.'

Another of Robert's favourite spaces is the dining room, where he has a turn-of-the-19th century chunky oak dining table with seven

leaves, surrounded by country oak chairs from the early 1900s. 'The table is 12 feet long and is great for dinner parties. On the walls I have a collection of framed historic photographs and paintings of Los Angeles.'

When Robert inherited the house, with it came some furniture. He has pieces from the American Federal period (early to mid-19th century), which coincided with the British Regency era. 'American Federal is simple and classic in woods such as mahogany, walnut, oak and cherry, and the style fits well with today's taste for more pared-back room schemes.'

The McNellis family collection also includes some 19th century Eastlake period items, a genre of furniture inspired by the English designer and architect Charles Eastlake who advocated an Arts &

Crafts-esque spirit of simplicity over high Victorian style. Two special ladies' desks – one in oak, the other in walnut – owned by Robert have an element of both, made in ornately carved timber but rounded off with original Eastlake decorative metal hinges, handles and locks. He is also fond of an Eastlake carved walnut china cabinet that has its original glass.

Stepping further back in time, Robert has some older pieces that he enjoys having around him. 'I have an American Hepplewhite design maple sideboard, c1825, that I acquired at an estate auction in Ohio in the 1980s. It is completely handmade, and a work of consummate craftsmanship. Plus an early 19th century American Sheraton design maple highboy [equivalent to a 'tallboy' chest of drawers in British parlance] which needs restoration but which I acquired for very little.'

With such an 'eye', honed over many years, Robert is well qualified to advise on how to shop for antiques: 'Antique fairs and shops are good places to learn the value, style and history of period pieces, but understandably prices will be higher. If you have the time to go to auctions and yard or boot sales these are often the best places to find great bargains and under-priced treasures. Occasionally I shop abroad but sometimes the cost of shipping negates the savings. Instead I prefer to buy from accredited importers because the items are already authenticated and in good condition.'

Karen and Martin Fry

04

Karen and Martin Fry moved to the Charente in Southwest France from the UK a few years ago. They live in a modern townhouse, with three bedrooms, a kitchen and a living room, artfully decorated in chalky whites and dove greys, with rugs across the wooden and terracotta tiled floors. The overall look is rustic and stylish, with a great mix of mostly French antiques.

The couple used to run an antiques shop together in London and have always loved plain country furniture, folk art and *objets d'art* both to own and to sell. 'Our style has evolved together over the seven years we've been married,' says Karen. 'We like a mix of functionality and stylishness and for the look to be quite playful – we've got a weathervane on the wall for example.'

Martin got into antiques in his thirties and started to attend auctions around the south coast of England. 'I didn't know much about it, but I started to learn and pick up a few pieces. Now I'm always on the hunt for things, I can't stop myself!' For many years Karen ran a shop in the New Forest specialising in country furniture.

They have found the Charente and surrounding regions a happy hunting ground for country antiques and vintage furniture. 'What attracts us first is the shape of something,' says Martin, 'and we try to buy things that weren't necessarily made for a purpose, like using an Edwardian bistro table as a bedside table. If we buy inexpensive 19th century "brown" furniture we tend to paint it a pale colour, or bleach it

down with a specialist wood bleach solution. The only exception to this would be dark-stained oak country furniture of the 17th and 18th centuries.'

The couple like to furnish their home with antiques for various reasons. Says Karen, 'First, they have a sense of age that you can't get with modern furniture – we have a tatty antique armchair but we just put a throw over it. Antiques bring individuality to a home and enable you to design your own look. Secondly, they are green and good for the environment. Lastly, they always have a resale value if you want to change your furnishings around and trade them in.'

As 'InsideOutdoors' Karen and Martin attend fairs several times a year in the UK (Chelsea Flower Show, Salvo Fair and Spirit of Christmas) and France (Isle-sur-la-Sorgue), bringing with them French pieces such as early 20th century Tolix pressed steel furniture, shutters and folk art. 'We never buy anything that we don't love ourselves,' says Karen, 'and we argue all the time – if I get a nice thing I want to keep it for our own home.' And would they ever buy new furniture for themselves? 'Oh no,' says Karen firmly, 'old is far more interesting.'

10

Places to visit and fairs

Places to visit and fairs

To appreciate antique furniture in more depth there is no substitute for visiting collections. You'll see the harmony of the design, for example; the colour, grain and figure of the wood; the carved ornamentation, motifs and gilding; and the all-important proportions. The fact that antiques held in collections are often of the highest quality should not put you off. While they might be out of reach financially, they tell us much about the design history of furniture and the skills of the people who made it. Here is a small selection of some interesting historic houses and museums.

Historic houses to visit

Blackwell, Cumbria, UK (www.blackwell.org.uk) The Arts & Crafts house Blackwell was designed by the renowned architect Mackay Hugh Baillie Scott and completed in 1900. Now owned by the Lakeland Arts Trust, the house has many fine pieces of Arts & Crafts furniture and simple country furniture, including pieces by Morris & Co, F A Voysey and Ernest Gimson.

Brush-Everard House, Williamsburg, Virginia, USA (www.history.org) Williamsburg, the 18th century capital of Virginia, has many restored period houses to explore such as the Brush-Everard House, built in 1718 by the local gunsmith and armourer John Brush, and purchased by public servant Thomas Everard in the mid-1750s. Inside, the weatherboarded house appears as it did in 1773 when Thomas lived there with his two daughters. The furniture is a blend of quality English and American antiques, providing a comparison of the two styles.

Castle Coole, County Fermanagh, Northern Ireland (www. nationaltrust.org.uk)
The Earls of Belmore spared no expense on their Neo-Classical mansion near Lough Coole, completed in 1798 and designed by James Wyatt. The rooms are Regency in style and include a sumptuous state bedroom prepared for George IV plus a suite of below-stairs rooms.

Fairbanks House, Dedham, Massachusetts, USA
(www.fairbankshouse.org) The Fairbanks House is thought to be the oldest surviving timber-frame house in North America. Constructed by East Anglian housewrights in the late 1630s, it was built for the puritan Jonathan Fairbanks, originally from Yorkshire in England. The house displays furniture collected over several generations, including an original carved oak and white pine chest as well as a maple gate-leg table, c1700, and some ladderback chairs from a similar period. The nearby Dedham Historical Society holds more important pieces of early American furniture.

Fairfax House, York, UK (www.fairfaxhouse.co.uk) This 18th century townhouse was designed as a winter home for Viscount Fairfax and his family by the distinguished architect John Carr. The Georgian house is fully furnished with an outstanding assembly of furniture, clocks, paintings and porcelain of the period.

Georgian House, Edinburgh, Scotland, UK (www.nts.org.uk)
The squares and crescents of Edinburgh's New Town reflect the

fashion for elegant, Neo-Classical architecture in the late 18th century. Renowned Scottish architect Robert Adam designed the townhouses on the north side of Charlotte Square in 1791. Number 7 is now under the care of the National Trust for Scotland and known as the Georgian House, where visitors can potter through the restored rooms filled with antique furnishings, fixtures and fittings.

Harewood House, Yorkshire, UK (www.harewood.org) 18th century Harewood House has one of the finest collections of Chippendale furniture, commissioned especially for the house. Highlights include the pier mirrors in the Yellow Drawing Room, Chinese-style lacquer furniture in the East Bedroom, the Diana and Minerva commode in the State Bedroom, and carved pelmets that resemble sumptuous fabric in the gallery.

Hill House, Glasgow, UK (www.nts.org.uk) Charles Rennie Mackintosh was commissioned to create this unique house in 1902 by book publisher Walter Blackie. Built in sandstone and in the architectural tradition of Scottish baronial properties, it is considered the architect's finest domestic design. Rennie Mackintosh and his wife Margaret Macdonald also designed the furniture and fittings, including the iconic high-backed chairs.

Karen Blixen Museum at Rungstedlund, Rungsted, Denmark (www.karen-blixen.dk) This is the house that Danish author Karen Blixen lived in from when she was writing *Out of Africa* until her death in 1961. Preserved as it was while she was living there, the original furniture includes 19th century tables and chairs, astragal-glazed cabinets, a white-painted Danish grandfather clock, and a number of beautiful old stoves or *kakelungnar*.

Kelmscott Manor, Oxfordshire, UK (www.kelmscottmanor.org.uk) Close to the River Thames in Kelmscott village is the place that inspired the 19th century designer William Morris, founder of the Arts & Crafts movement. Kelmscott, a Grade I listed farmhouse dating to around 1600, was Morris's summer home, which he shared with his wife and children and the artist Dante Gabriel Rossetti. The house holds a collection of period furniture, ceramics and textiles, all family-owned, and is a reflection of their simple, harmonious taste. Morris is buried in the village church.

Knole, Kent, UK (www.nationaltrust.org.uk) A Kentish ragstone manor house set in a magnificent medieval deer park, Knole has been impressing visitors for over 500 years. Within the 13 state rooms is a world-renowned collection of 17th century royal furniture from the Stuart period, featuring rare original *passementerie* (or trimmings). You'll also see a prototype for the Knole settee.

Lilla Hyttnäs, Sundborn, Sweden (www.clg.se) The influential Swedish artists Carl Larsson and his wife Karin came to live at Lilla Hyttnäs – 'the little hut on a point' – in 1888. The 19th century farmhouse was where the couple raised their eight children, immortalised in Larsson's depictions of domestic life. Original interiors on show today, courtesy of the Larsson Family Trust, are a blend of styles. The elegant, airy drawing room is inspired by 18th century provincial Gustavian style, while the vibrant dining room has red-painted furniture, considered undignified at the time.

Mr Straw's House, Nottinghamshire, UK (www.nationaltrust.org.uk/mr-straws-house) This semi-detached house in the town of Worksop shows life as experienced by a middling family, whose head of household was a grocer. The Straws lived in this house from the 1920s, until the National Trust was bequeathed the property and its contents in the early 1990s. It is a time capsule of conservative 1920s style, with rooms largely furnished with Victorian furniture.

Number 1 Royal Crescent, Bath, UK (www.bath-preservation-trust.org.uk) One of 30 houses that make up stunning Royal Crescent, created between 1767 and 1774 by the Wood family, Number 1 has been restored to its late 18th century finery. The decoration and furnishings give an authentic flavour of how people would have lived in the house during the Bath socialising 'season' from October to June. See a

gallery houses the decorative objects, paintings and furniture collected by him over half a century until his death in 1925. A renowned collection of 18th century furniture features pieces made by the best cabinet-makers – Mayhew & Ince, John Linnell and Thomas Chippendale. There is also a collection of French furniture and memorabilia associated with Napoleon.

MAK, Vienna, Austria (www.mak.at) The Austrian Museum of Applied Arts (MAK) is a broad-ranging collection with an extensive holding of antique furniture. The main focuses of the display are Baroque and Rococo, Empire and Biedermeier, and Art Nouveau. See everything from complete period rooms saved from the scrapheap to individual antique pieces. One highlight is an overview of 100 years of Thonet bentwood furniture production.

Metropolitan Museum of Art, New York, NY, USA (www.metmuseum. org) The Met has a superb collection of furniture, ranging from the 17th to the 20th centuries. Most of the 2,000-plus pieces on display are American in origin, and give an opportunity to see how makers were influenced by European styles, and developed their own traits. A selection of Arts & Crafts furniture includes chests, tables, chairs and clocks made by Gustav Stickley, a leading light in the American Arts & Crafts movement. See also magnificent rooms saved from English aristocratic houses, such as Croome Court, Lansdowne House and Kirtlington Park.

Musée des Arts Décoratifs, Paris, France (www.lesartsdecoratifs.fr) On rue de Rivoli close to the Seine, this museum holds a collection of French furniture, tableware, carpets and glass pieces ranging from the 20th back to the 13th century. The gallery has period rooms on display that include part of French fashion designer Jeanne Lanvin's house from the early 1920s, a dining room from the late 1800s, and the bedroom of a courtesan from 1875 among others.

Museum für Angewandte Kunst (MAKK), Cologne, Germany (www.museenkoeln.de) This museum of applied arts has a huge collection of furniture, carpets, tableware and other decorative objects dating from the 10th century to the present. The best European manufacturers are represented within the collection so expect a comprehensive 'tour' of design developments over the centuries.

Museum of Fine Arts, Boston, Massachusetts, USA (www.mfa.org) This is the place to see a comprehensive collection of mostly American-made furniture from the 17th to the 19th centuries. See chairs, tables and sofas made in native woods, maple, walnut, pine and oak by furniture makers from New England, New York, and Pennsylvania. Uniquely American styles such as a late 18th century 'Lolling chair' sit alongside candle tables, curvaceous chests and ornamental mirrors.

Nagytétény Castle Museum, Budapest, Hungary (www.nagytetenyi.hu) The beautifully restored 18th century Rudnyánsky Castle is home to a permanent exhibition, 'The history of furniture art', featuring pieces held by Budapest's Museum of Applied Arts. Within the Baroque castle's 27 rooms, visitors can view some 300 items, dating from 1440s Gothic style to the 1850s Biedermeier look. See craftsman-made chests, cabinets, wardrobes, armchairs and sewing tables, plus much more.

Philadelphia Museum of Art, Philadelphia, Pennsylvania, USA (www.philamuseum.org) The Philadelphia Museum of Art, housed in a Greek Revival building, is renowned for its paintings. It also holds a superb collection of Philadelphian and Pennsylvanian furniture and silver of the 18th and 19th centuries. Like the Met in New York, it has whole rooms salvaged from English houses, such as the 18th century drawing room from Lansdowne House, designed by Robert Adam.

Temple Newsam House, Leeds, UK (www.leeds.gov.uk/templenewsam) This Tudor-Jacobean mansion was bought in 1922 by Leeds City Council and transformed into a nationally important collection of decorative arts. Thirty original interiors are decked out with paintings, porcelain, textiles, silver and sumptuous wallpapers. On display is important furniture from England, Europe and the Orient, including Tudor and Stuart pieces, and a fine collection of 18th century pieces by cabinet-makers such as Giles Grendey and Thomas Chippendale.

Thonet Museum, Frankenberg, Germany (www.thonet.de)
At Thonet's Frankenberg headquarters, founded in 1889, is a family-curated museum with a definitive collection of the furniture designed by Michael Thonet and his descendants, gathered from around the world. Thonet bentwood pieces, such as the original Chair No 14 (now referred to as Chair No 214) first produced in 1859, are still in production at the factory.

Victoria and Albert Museum, London, UK (www.vam.ac.uk) The V&A has a renowned collection of furniture representing many periods and styles. Highlights include the furniture shown in the British Galleries, particularly Room 125, which contains the work of William Morris, Christopher Dresser and Charles Rennie Mackintosh; Room 122 which assesses the impact on design of the Gothic Revival in the 19th century; also unmissable is Room 52, which houses the magnificent mid-18th century panelled Music Room saved from Norfolk House in St James's when it was demolished in 1938. A recently opened Furniture Gallery showcases 200 outstanding examples of British, European, American and Asian furniture representing 600 years of design history.

Wallace Collection, London, UK (www.wallacecollection.org) A small museum of European standing, the Wallace Collection is housed in an aristocratic London townhouse. Among paintings by Fragonard and Watteau, Sèvres porcelain and ranks of shiny armour, find glorious 18th century French furniture amassed by the Marquesses of Hertford and their scion Sir Richard Wallace. There are more than 500 pieces in the collection, including a rare selection of furniture by pre-eminent French cabinet-maker André Boulle who specialised in marquetry.

Winterthur, Wilmington, Delaware, USA (www.winterthur.org) The 175-room mansion Winterthur (pronounced 'winter-tour') houses the largest collection of American furniture in the US, dating from around 1640 to 1860. In the 1920s Henry Francis du Pont, a scion of the prominent du Pont family, began collecting American Windsor chairs, painted chests and simple pine and maple furniture, progressing to some of the finest New England and Philadelphian furniture ever made, plus high quality pieces from the Federal and Empire periods (1790s to the 1830s). Sixty years ago he graciously put his 9,000-strong collection on display to the public at his childhood home, Winterthur.

Wycombe Museum, Buckinghamshire, UK (www.wycombe.gov.uk/museum) The museum charts the history of furniture making over several centuries in the Buckinghamshire area, the centre of English Windsor chair making in the 19th century. There's a comprehensive collection of Windsor chairs from the 18th to the 20th centuries, and examples of simple country rush and cane chairs. Visitors can also see the tools used by the itinerant wood turners known as 'bodgers' who worked in the nearby beech woods, turning stretchers and legs for chairs that were then sold on to local workshops. See also the tools of the pit-sawyers who cut the planks that were made into seats.

 NEED TO KNOW: *KNOWLEDGE AT YOUR FINGERTIPS*

Britain's National Trust recently launched a new research tool covering its historic properties in England, Wales and Northern Ireland. A free-to-use database of all collections, including furniture, means that you can search by period, by house, by maker, by category of item, and by type of material to find specific antiques and where to see them. The project took ten years to complete and lists nearly 50,000 items of period furniture alone. Log on to www.nationaltrustcollections.org.uk to see what you can find.

January

BRAFA (Brussels Antiques & Fine Arts Fair), Tour & Taxis, Avenue du Port 86 C, 1000 Brussels, Belgium (www.brafa.be) This annual fair attracts exhibitors from around the world. Find top quality antique furniture dating from the Middle Ages onwards.

Winter Decorative Antiques & Textiles Fair, Battersea Evolution, Battersea Park, London, UK (www.decorativefair.com) 140 specialist dealers from around Europe encompassing many periods and styles.

The National Fine Arts & Antiques Fair, The NEC, Birmingham, UK(www.thenationalfair.co.uk) One of the year's most prestigious antiques fairs outside London.

Luxury Antiques and Fine Art Fair, The Mere, Knutsford, Cheshire, UK (www.merefair.com) A small upmarket fair of 30 dealers offering a good range of antique furniture as well as objects and paintings.

Winter Antiques Show, Park Avenue Armory, New York, NY, USA (www.winterantiquesshow.com) A prestigious 10-day annual fair bringing together antiques from dealers around the USA.

The NYC Metro Show, Metropolitan Pavilion, 125 West 18th Street, New York, NY, USA (www.metroshownyc.com) A four-day event of 30 or so folk art and Americana specialists.

February

Penman Petersfield Fair, The Festival Hall, Heath Road, Petersfield, Hampshire, UK (www.penman-fairs.co.uk) A twice-yearly fair that attracts over 50 dealers known for quality and value.

Luxury Antiques Weekend, Tortworth Court, near Wotton-under-Edge, South Gloucestershire, UK (www.tortworthcourtfair.com) A boutique-style fair representing 22 dealers offering a select range of antique furniture as well as objects and paintings.

Penman Chesterfield Show, County Grandstand, Chester Racecourse, Cheshire, UK (www.penman-fairs.co.uk) 50 stands of antiques and art at this twice-yearly show; members of BADA and LAPADA strongly represented.

The Original Miami Beach Antique Show, Miami Beach Convention Center, Miami, FL, USA (www.originalmiamibeachantiqueshow.com)

800 dealers from around the globe offering everything from jewellery and silverware to furniture.

Antikmässan, Stockholmsmässan, Älvsjö, Stockholm, Sweden (www.antikmassan.se) A renowned annual four-day fair, held in association with the Swedish Art & Antique Dealer's Assocation (SKAF), selling Nordic antiques and fine arts from 250 dealers.

Montpellier, Parc des Expositions, Montpellier, Languedoc Roussillon, France (cipolat.com) Held three times a year, in February, April and July. Dealers from all over Europe attend, offering a broad selection of quality antiques.

Modenantiquaria, viale Virgilio, 41123 Modena, Italy (www.modenantiquaria.it) An upmarket, annual nine-day fair includes dealers offering everything from fine European furniture to paintings, bronzes, ceramics and tapestries, from the Renaissance period to Art Deco.

March

The Chelsea Antiques Fair, Chelsea Old Town Hall, King's Road, Chelsea, London, UK (www.penman-fairs.co.uk) The twice-yearly Chelsea Fair is the oldest antiques fair in Britain. Enjoy the relaxed approach of the boutique-style fair and 36 vetted exhibitors who bring porcelain, silver and paintings as well as furniture.

Luxury Antiques Weekend, Linden Hall, near Morpeth, Northumberland, UK (www.lindenhallfair.com) 26 dealers who are members of BADA and LAPADA offering fine antique furniture, objects and paintings.

BADA Antiques & Fine Art Fair, Duke of York Square, Chelsea, London, UK (www.bada-antiques-fair.co.uk) BADA members deal in prestigious antiques, so expect to see pieces such as authentic Chippendale furniture at this annual, week-long show attended by 100 dealers.

TEFAF Maastricht, The MECC (Maastricht Exhibition & Congress Centre), Maastricht, The Netherlands (www.tefaf.com) A 10-day extravaganza of high quality art and antiques presented by 260 dealers from 16 countries – one of the most prestigious shows in the world.

The Pier Antiques Show, Pier 94, 12th Avenue, New York, NY, USA (www.stellashows.com) A fashionable mix of vintage and traditional antiques, art, jewellery and collectables presented by 500 dealers over two days.

Connecticut Spring Antiques Show, Connecticut Expo Center, Hartford, CT, USA (www.ctspringantiquesshow.com) Over 70 dealers offering American-made furniture pre-dating 1840.

Antikmässan i Brösarp, Brösarps Gästgiveri, Brösarp Österlen, Skåne, Sweden (www.osterlen-runt.se/365) An annual three-day antiques fair held in this small Swedish village deep in the Skåne region – *Wallander* country – with stands featuring the wares of over 40 dealers.

Russian Antique Salon, 10 Krymsky val, Central House of Artists, Moscow 119049, Russia (www.antiquesalon.ru) Held twice a year in March and October with over 200 stands offering a wide range of 18th and 19th century artworks and fine antiques.

April

The Antique Fair Prague, Novom stská Radnice exhibition hall, Prague, The Czech Republic (www.asociace.com) Held in April and November, attended by over 60 Czech dealers offering furniture, ceramics, glass, textiles and art.

Spring Decorative Antiques & Textiles Fair, Battersea Evolution, London, UK (www.decorativefair.com) A wide spectrum of British, French, Scandinavian and Eastern European antique furniture with many different periods and styles from 140 specialist dealers.

Antiques for Everyone Spring Fair, The NEC Birmingham, UK (www. antiquesforeveryone.co.uk) The largest vetted antiques fair in the UK, which happens three times a year with over 300 dealers, many specialising in period furniture.

International Antiques Fair, Isle-sur-la-Sorgue, Provence, France (www. foireantiquites-islesurlasorgue.fr) In addition to the 250 antiques shops based permanently in the town, there is an internationally renowned antiques fair twice a year, at Easter and in August. During the four-day fair, over 200 dealers offer affordable furniture.

The Art & Antique Fair Lisbon, Cordoaria Nacional building, Avenida da India, 1300 Lisbon, Portugal (www.apa.pt) An annual 10-day fair bringing together 29 members of the Portuguese Dealer's Association, offering an upmarket variety of regional and European art and antiques.

The Philadelphia Antiques Show, Pennsylvania Convention Center, Philadelphia, PA, USA (www.philaantiques.com) The four-day annual show is renowned for its selection of Americana and folk art, and English and Continental antiques from 50 dealers.
Montpellier, Parc des Expositions. See February.

May

Guildford Antiques & Art Fair, G-Live, London Road, Guildford, Surrey (www.penman-fairs.co.uk) Features 46 dealers, with a good showing from the West Country and the southeast, offering a wide range of antique furniture.
Thames Valley Antique Dealers' Association (TVADA) Spring Antiques Fair, Stubbings Estate, near Maidenhead, Berkshire, UK (www.tvada.co.uk) Over 35 dealers and specialists from the Thames Valley region offering a mix of antique furniture, fine art, rugs and collectables.

June

Olympia International Fine Art & Antiques Fair, Olympia, London, UK (www.olympia-art-antiques.com) This is a ten-day, fully vetted annual event supported by BADA and LAPADA. 150 dealers offer a huge variety of antique furniture, art and objects.
Cressing Antiques & Art Fair, Cressing Temple, Witham Road, Cressing, nr Braintree, Essex, UK (www.penman-fairs.co.uk) An architectural treat, the fair is held in two ancient 13th century barns. Find wares from 30 antiques dealers on offer, plus a smaller section of contemporary art.
Art Antiques London, Albert Memorial West Lawn, Kensington Gardens, London, UK (www.haughton.com) The week-long fair incorporates the International Ceramics Fair and presents over 70 leading art, ceramics and antiques dealers.
Salvo Fair, Knebworth House, Hertfordshire, UK (www.salvo-fair.com) Alongside reclaimed building materials are period furnishings and accessories, such as church furniture, sofas and chairs, and French country pieces from over 70 salvage yards and specialist dealers.

July

Antiques for Everyone Summer Fair, NEC Birmingham, UK (www.antiquesforeveryone.co.uk) See April.
Montpellier, Parc des Expositions. See February.

August

Maine Antiques Festival, The Fairgrounds, Union, ME, USA (www.maineantiquefest.com) A three-day gathering held annually of around 200 dealers from across the US and Canada, offering furniture from formal style to country looks.
International Antiques Fair, Isle-sur-la-Sorgue, Provence, France (www.foireantiquites-islesurlasorgue.fr) See April.
Brocanters Menorca, Recinto Ferial de Es Mercadal, Migjorn Gran, 33 Es Mercadal, Spain (http://es.neventum.com/brocanters-menorca/2012). The historic Balearic island's annual fair held in early August, where a number of dealers showcase antique furniture, collectables and *objets d'art*.

September

The Lapada Art & Antiques Fair, Berkeley Square, London, UK (www.lapadalondon.com) A glorious range of top quality antique furniture, art and jewellery. Some smaller more affordable items available too if you hunt at the annual six-day fair.
The Chelsea Antiques Fair, Chelsea Old Town Hall, King's Road, Chelsea, London, UK (www.penman-fairs.co.uk) See March.
Penman Petersfield Fair, The Festival Hall, Heath Road, Petersfield, Hampshire (www.penman-fairs.co.uk) See February.
Luxury Antiques Weekend, Stapleford Park, near Melton Mowbray, Leicestershire, UK (www.staplefordparkfair.com) An upmarket, boutique fair presenting 21 dealers, many members of BADA and LAPADA, offering a select range of antique furniture as well as objects and paintings.
Biennale des Antiquaires, Grand Palais, Paris, France (www.sna-france.com)

Held in the glass-roofed Grand Palais, built for the Universal Exhibition of 1900, the biennial 10-day fair attracts the cream of French and European antiques dealers. The next one is in 2014, then 2016 and so on. Also look out for the Salon du Collectionneur, also run by the Syndicat National des Antiquaires.

Braderie de Lille, Lille, France (www.lilletourism.com) The annual two-day flea market claims to be the biggest in Europe, with 10,000 vendors lining the city centre streets.

Cremona Antiquaria, Cremona Fiere, Cremona, Emilia-Romagna, Italy (www.cremonafiere.it) An upmarket eight-day show offering a wide range of European furniture, artworks, carpets, and more for sale.

October

Pays d'Aix-Marseille Antiques Fair, Hall 1, Park Chanot, Marseilles, France (www.salondesantiquaires.fr/antiques-fair-france.php) Over 80 antiques dealers from all over France selling quality antique furniture and decorative arts dating from the 17th to early 20th centuries.

Autumn Decorative Antiques & Textiles Fair, Battersea Evolution, London, UK (www.decorativefair.com) A wide spectrum of British, French, Scandinavian and Eastern European antique furniture encompassing many different periods and styles from 140 specialist dealers.

Penman Chesterfield Show, County Grandstand, Chester Racecourse, Cheshire (www.penman-fairs.co.uk) See February.

Antiques for Everyone Winter Fair, NEC Birmingham, UK (www.antiquesforeveryone.co.uk) See April.

The Esher Hall Antiques and Fine Art Fair, Esher Hall, Sandown Park Racecourse, Esher, Surrey, UK (www.esherhallfair.com) An upmarket fair of 40 dealers offering a good range of antique furniture, objects and paintings.

The San Francisco Fall Antiques Show, Festival Pavilion, Fort Mason Center, San Francisco, CA, USA (www.sffas.org) A West Coast highlight, the four-day annual fair attracts over 70 dealers offering American, English and Continental antique furniture, art and porcelain.

The International Fine Art & Antique Dealers Show, The Park Avenue Armory, Park Avenue at 67th Street, New York, NY, USA (www. haughton.com) An upmarket fair featuring over 60 dealers from America, UK, France and other European countries.

Antiques Fairs in Umbria in various towns including Perugia, Spoleto and Todi, Italy (www.umbriavacanza.co.uk) Small monthly fairs dotted around the main towns of Umbria; find Italian collectables and linen, and smaller items of furniture.

Verzamelen in Stijl, Dam 9, Amsterdam 1012 JS, The Netherlands (www.verzameleninstijl.nl) Around 40 Dutch dealers specialising in smaller antique furnishings such as clocks, mirrors, rugs, writing slopes, plus ceramics, statues and jewellery.

Russian Antique Salon. See March.

November

Antique Fair Prague. See April.

Winter Fine Art & Antiques Fair, Olympia, London, UK (www.olympia-antiques.com) Supported by BADA and LAPADA, the week-long fair offers a great range of antique furniture from some of the 140 dealers who attend.

Koelnmesse, Messehochhaus, Cologne, Germany (www.cofaa.com) In the heart of the Rhineland, the annual Cologne Fine Art & Antiques fair includes over 100 mainly German dealers, who offer art, furniture and decorative antiques with a northern European flavour.

Feriarte Art and Antiques Fair, Hall 3, Feria de Madrid, Madrid, Spain (www.ifema.es) An annual nine-day gathering of over 125 Spanish and international dealers, showcasing the best European antiques. Also strong in 19th century paintings, lamps, sculpture and clocks.

December

Guildford Christmas Antiques & Art Fair, G-Live, London Road, Guildford, Surrey (www.penman-fairs.co.uk) A two-day fair with a focus on Christmas gifts and antique treats.

NEED TO KNOW: *IACF ANTIQUES FAIRS*

Anyone who likes antiques hunting is likely to come across the International Antiques and Collectors (IACF) Fairs held six times a year at Newark in Nottinghamshire, five times a year at Ardingly in West Sussex and Shepton Mallet in Somerset, plus several other less frequent locations. With up to 4,000 stands, Newark is the biggest fair and pulls in buyers from all over the UK and abroad attracted by keen prices for antique furniture and much more. The website (iacf.co.uk) offers a year planner to download, featuring all the upcoming fair dates.

INSTANT EXPERT: *FIND MORE FAIRS*

- **UK:** For information on many more small fairs held across the UK and Ireland log onto the website Antiques Atlas (www.antiques-atlas.com), which carries a comprehensive month-by-month listing of local fairs and entry/location details.
- **USA:** For details of fairs held across the USA, visit the website Calendar of Art & Antiques (www.calendarofantiques.com) which offers a similar month-by-month listing for fairs such as the regular Brimfield Antique Show in Massachusetts, and the Vermont Antiques Dealers' Association's (VADA) Annual Antiques Show.
- **France:** For info on French brocantes and flea markets go to the website Antiquités en France (www.antiquites-en-france.com) for a region-by-region guide. For info on the huge weekend Paris antiques and flea market Marché aux Puces St-Ouen de Clignancourt go to www.parispuces.com; and for Paris's Marché aux Puces de la Porte de Vanves, check out www.pucesdevanves.typepad.com.
- **Europe:** The Kunstpedia Foundation, a fine arts volunteer organisation, is dedicated to sharing information about arts and culture events. Its website carries many listings, including a selection of antiques fairs around Europe. Find them at (www.kunstpedia.com/art-and-antique-fairs.html.

Picture credits

Every effort has been made to credit the appropriate source, but if you find any errors or omissions please notify us. We will ensure that they are corrected in any subsequent printing.

All courtesy of The Decorative Antiques & Textiles Fair: pp 13, 15, 17, 37, 60, 66 (top), 67 (top), 73, 74, 81, 86, 92, 102, 113, 125, 128, 129, 132-137, 145, 146, 148, 150, 151, 153.
All courtesy of Dreweatts: pp 25, 27-29, 31, 32, 61-65, 66 (bottom), 69, 71, 72, 75-80, 82-85, 93-96 (top), 97-101, 105, 106, 108, 110, 112, 114, 115, 123, 124, 138, 144, 147, 149, 152,
All courtesy of Lyon & Turnbull: pp 46, 49, 50, 53, 55, 67, 87, 103, 107, 109, 120-122, 131

GAP Interiors/Mark Nicholson, **pp 10, 59, 163, 164**; courtesy of J Collins & Son, **p 14**; courtesy of Country Oak Antiques, **p 18**; Copyright Dean and Chapter of Westminster, **p 22**; GAP Interiors/Bruce Hemming, **p 41**; GAP Interiors/ Piotr Gesicki, **p 91**; GAP Interiors/Douglas Gibb, **p 119**; GAP Interiors/Guillaume de Laubier, **p 143**; GAP Interiors/Bill Kingston, **p 157**; GAP Interiors/Mark Bolton, **p 158**; Picture by M0tty, **p 159**; courtesy of Bee Good (www.beegood.net), **p 160**; courtesy of Suzandy Caning & Furniture (www.suzandy.co.uk), **p 162**; © Photographer: Helen Toresdotter, **pp 168-173**; © Photographer: David Killingback (www.davidkillingback.com), **pp 174-178**; Photographer: Fernando Escovar, **pp 180, 182-185**; courtesy of *Period Living*/ photographer: Lydia Evans, **pp 186, 187, 188 (top right), 189**; courtesy of *Period Living*/ photographer: Elin Eriksen, **p 188 (top left and bottom right)**; courtesy Karen Blixen Museet/ photographer: Jens Lindhe.

Chapter opening drawings: © Louisa Jones

Acknowledgements

For help in sourcing images my special thanks to Dreweatts Fine Art Auction Group (dnfa.com), Lyon & Turnbull auction house (lyonandturnbull.com) and The Decorative Antiques & Textiles Fair (decorativefair.com).

For background information and historical context thanks to Lapada and The Decorative Antiques & Textiles Fair; antiques dealers Circa 1900, J Collins & Son, Country Oak Antiques, Courtyard Antiques (Brasted), Guy Dennler Antiques, Anthony Fell, Sue Killinger Antiques, Lennox Cato, M Charpentier Antiques, The Swan at Tetsworth, Quiet Street Antiques, WA Pinn & Sons Antiques and Welsh Antiques; the Victoria and Albert Museum and the Geffrye Museum of the Home, both London; the National Trust (England, Wales & Northern Ireland) and the National Trust for Scotland; Salvo Fair, Thornton Kay and Ruby Hazael; Pippa Roberts at Pippa Roberts PR; Period Living magazine; Homes & Antiques magazine.

I'm grateful to my case studies Bengt Lindvall and Lennart Svensson, Sarah Florence Saumarez, Robert McNellis, and Karen and Martin Fry for time freely given.

On a personal note, thanks to my parents, Jill and Mike, and my parents in law, Jean and Mike, whose furniture and good taste we continue to enjoy.

Index